KT-244-371

PROCEEDINGS

OF THE

GENERAL COURT MARTIAL

ON

CAPTAIN WATHEN, 15th KINGS HUSSARS

A FACSIMILE REPRINT

PUBLISHED BY FREDERICK MULLER LTD

First Published in Great Britain, 1834, by Roake and Varty
This facsimile edition published in 1970 by
Frederick Muller Ltd., Fleet Street, London, E.C.4.

Reproduced and Printed in Great Britain by
Redwood Press Limited, Trowbridge and London

SBN 584:10906:7

PROCEEDINGS

OF THE

GENERAL COURT MARTIAL

UPON THE

TRIAL OF CAPTAIN WATHEN,

FIFTEENTH KING'S HUSSARS.

LONDON:
ROAKE AND VARTY, 31, STRAND.
1834.

COURT MARTIAL.

At a General Court Martial, held at Cork, on Monday, the 23rd day of December, 1833, and continued by adjournment, in pursuance of a warrant from Lieut.-General the Right Hon. Sir Hussey Vivian, Bart. K.C.B. commanding his Majesty's Forces in that part of the United Kingdom called Ireland, bearing date the 16th day of December, 1833, being thereunto authorised by a warrant from his Majesty, dated the 25th day of April, 1833.

PRESIDENT,

Major-General Sir John Buchan, K.C.B.

MEMBERS,

Lieut.-Col. J. C. Chatterton, K.H. 4th Drag. Guards.
Lieut.-Col. James L. Basden, C.B. 89th Regiment.
Brevet-Major C. Bridge, Royal Artillery.
Major William Mitchell, 56th Depôt.
Capt. A. J. Aplin, 89th Reg.
Capt. E. B. Curteis, 7th Drag. Guards.
Lieut. C. G. King, 89th Regiment.
Lieut.-Col. H. White, 96th Depôt.
Lieut.-Col. R. Anderson, 91st Regiment.
Major John Kelly, 24th Depôt.
Major John Walter, 29th Depôt.
Capt. Francis Hawkins, 89th Regiment.
Capt. Warburton Grey, 56th Depôt.
Lieut. Ralph P. Ince, 56th Depôt.

David Walker, Esq.
Deputy Judge Advocate General, and Judge Martial.

The Court being assembled, the warrants being read, and the prisoner having no objection to offer to any of the members.

The several members of the Court being duly sworn, and the Judge-Advocate also sworn,

Captain Augustus Wathen, of the 15th Hussars, came prisoner before the Court, and the following charges were exhibited against him :—

1st. For that he, Captain Wathen, of the 15th Hussars, did, on the 8th of November, 1833, at Cork, at the half-yearly inspection of the 15th Hussars, voluntarily state, in an invidious and improper manner, to Major-General Sir Thomas Arbuthnot, that an unusual supply of new stable-jackets had been issued to the men of his troop, and which had been sent from the tailor's shop without his knowledge; thereby imputing improper conduct to Lieutenant-Colonel Lord Brudenel, his commanding officer, although it is the custom of the service to issue new stable-jackets to cavalry soldiers as they may require them.

2nd. For conduct unbecoming the character of an officer and a gentleman in first having stated to Major-General Sir Thomas Arbuthnot, on Friday, the said 8th of November, at the place aforesaid, "that he had been informed by the serjeants of his troop, that the men were discontented at having new stable-jackets delivered out to them," such statement being contrary to the fact; and having afterwards, on the same day, in an improper and disrespectful manner, when addressed by the Major-General, denied having made the above statement, which denial he, Capt. Wathen, repeated to the Major-General, on the Monday following

3rd. For conduct unbecoming the character of an officer and a gentleman in stating to Major-Gen. Sir Thomas Arbuthnot, on the said 8th of November, at the place aforesaid, "that he had reported or mentioned to Lieutenant-Colonel Lord Brudenell, that the men of his troop had expressed discontent at having new stable-jackets delivered out to them," which statement was directly contrary to truth and fact.

4th. For conduct unbecoming the character of an officer and a gentleman, in having in a letter addressed to his said commanding officer, Lieutenant-Colonel Lord Brudenell, dated 12th November, 1833, made a statement contrary to truth and fact, viz. "that in compliance with instructions conveyed to him by the Adjutant on the evening of the said 8th of November, after the inspection, he had assembled his troop after evening stables, to convey to them the Major-General's approbation of their appearance, &c.," whereas he, Captain Wathen, did not on that evening obey Lieut.-Colonel Lord Brudenell's orders to the above effect, conveyed to him through the Adjutant.

5th. For that he, Captain Wathen, after having assembled the men of his troop, on Saturday, the 9th November, 1833, at the place aforesaid, addressed them in an irregular and unofficer-like manner, by then and there not confining himself to communicating to them the

Major-General's approbation of the regiment, but in adding that some strangers or civilians had particularly remarked the soldier-like appearance of his troop, or words to that effect, and also saying that he had no doubt that had they gone on service, they would have done their duty as well as any other troop, notwithstanding any unpleasant circumstances which had occurred in the troop," or words to that effect, which address was highly improper, inasmuch as allusion was therein made to Lieutenant-Colonel Lord Brudenell's recent censure on the want of attention to the care of the horses in Captain Wathen's troop.

6th. For having on the 12th of November, 1833, at the place aforesaid, refused to obey an order then given to him by Lieutenant-Colonel Lord Brudenell, his commanding officer, to repeat verbally what he had said to his men on the said Saturday, 9th of November, and in having afterwards, when permitted by his said commanding officer to commit to writing the nature of the said address to his troop, repeatedly refused to obey the order then and there verbally given to him by his said commanding officer, to leave his written statement locked up in the regimental office, during his absence at parade, such conduct as aforesaid, being insubordinate, unbecoming the character of an officer and a gentleman, to the prejudice of good order and military discipline, and in breach of the Articles of War.

The prisoner pleaded NOT GUILTY.

Lieutenant-Colonel Lord Brudenell, commanding the 15th Hussars, attended as prosecutor, and addressed the Court as follows:

MR. PRESIDENT AND GENTLEMEN,

It is with feelings of deep regret that I am compelled to appear before you this day, as the prosecutor of an officer under my command.

But however unwilling, under all the circumstances of the case about to be submitted to your investigation, I consider that I should not be conscientiously discharging the duties of the command entrusted to me, or furthering the good of the service, were I, from private considerations, to hesitate in coming forward on the present occasion, and laying the whole of Captain Wathen's conduct before you.

I beg to state, that if ever there was a case which required that calm and dispassionate consideration which it is sure to meet with before a court composed of officers, it is that which I am about to submit to you, after the unusual, and, I may say, unprecedented manner in which all the circumstances of the case have been misrepresented and prejudged by the public press.

Without accusing any individual, I must point out as a very extraordinary fact, that the most minute and circumstantial details of what took place at an interview between Captain Wathen and myself, in the regimental office of the 15th Hussars, on the 12th of November, at which the adjutant alone was present, appeared almost immediately afterwards in the newspapers of this town, but so garbled, and perverted, as to give the most favourable impression of the cause of that party for whom the press was evidently employed.

I shall now take the liberty of making a few observations on the six Charges which I have thought it my duty to prefer against Captain Wathen, upon the understanding that I shall not be precluded from giving my evidence on each of the Charges, should I desire it.

With regard to the first Charge, I shall leave it to Major-General Sir Thomas Arbuthnot, to describe the manner in which Captain Wathen's statement was made on the 8th of last month. I shall be able to show you that it is the custom of the service to issue new stable-jackets to cavalry soldiers as they may require them, and I shall also prove to you that it has been more or less the custom of this regiment; but even if I could not substantiate this fact, Captain Wathen would not have been justified in making that statement to the major-general, because provided I adhere to the rules, regulations, and customs of the service, I am not bound to follow precisely in the steps of my predecessor in command of this regiment.

With regard to the second, third, and fourth Charges, I have no observations at present to make; they are all for making statements contrary to truth and fact, and if I prove them, they require no comment from me.

With regard to the fifth Charge, I beg to point out that Captain Wathen assembled his troop at an unusual hour, and addressed them in an unofficerlike and irregular manner, stating that civilians and strangers had expressed approbation of his troop,—that the left troop of the line was particularly soldier-like in appearance,—that they were under orders for foreign service,—that he had no doubt they would be as brave a troop as any other troop,—that his heart would always be with them wherever they went,—that they would do their duty as well as any other troop, notwithstanding any unpleasant circumstances or unpleasantness, (or words to that effect,) which had occurred in the troop.

Now, sir, I beg to state that Captain Wathen was not justified in saying anything to his troop with regard to the approbation of civilians, that it was irregular and unnecessary to talk to his troop about their bravery on foreign service; because there never had been a question, nor could there be any doubt, as to the good conduct of any troop of the 15th Hussars on foreign service.

Then the unpleasant circumstances to which he referred, could, I assert, allude to nothing else but my strong and repeated censure of the want of care and attention to the grooming of the horses previous to the inspection of Captain Wathen's troop; disapprobation which I had expressed at almost every parade in watering order, on which occasions the troop horses are usually inspected.

Connecting this, sir, with Captain Wathen's statement to the Major-general on the preceding day (Friday, the 8th November) relative to the stable-jackets, I cannot imagine, any conduct on the part of an officer more calculated to create discontent amongst the men, and to bring the commanding officer's authority into contempt and disrepute.

With regard to the sixth charge, I shall be able to prove to you that after Captain Wathen had several times disobeyed my orders, he refused to leave a statement locked up with the regimental records during his absence at the parade, and to which he was to return to finish after the parade. He repeatedly, positively, and deliberately refused to obey my orders. I shall prove to you that I treated him with every forbearance, and showed every reluctance to place him in arrest; until then, I did not conceive it possible for any officer holding a commission in the service, so positively and deliberately to refuse to obey an order verbally given to him by his commanding officer, in direct breach of the 12th clause of the Article of War.

Major-General Sir Thomas Arbuthnot's evidence.

First witness for the Prosecution, Major-General Sir Thomas Arbuthnot, K. C. B., commanding the southern district, being duly sworn, was examined by the prosecutor, and the following questions were put to him.

Q. With regard to the three first charges, have the goodness to state what occurred in the regimental office of the 15th Hussars, at the inspection of the regiment on the 8th November last?

A. Having on the day mentioned in the first charge inspected the troop books of the 15th Hussars, Captain Wathen's being the last, I asked that officer the usual question, if he was in the habit of settling with the men himself at the end of each month? his reply was, "Yes, sir, I settle my own accounts," on which I remarked, "Captain Wathen, your books are made out quite correct, and I am satisfied with them in all respects." I then made a slight bow, conceiving that Captain Wathen would withdraw as the other officers had done, for I saw the troop books in succession; instead of this, however, Captain Wathen, addressing me, said, "General, I understand Lieutenant-Colonel Lord Brudenell has made a complaint to you respecting the amount of the debt of my troop, and I wish to offer some explanation on the subject." My reply was, "Captain Wathen, Lord Brudenell has made no such complaint to me. I have not yet examined the returns of the regiment, and I know nothing of the matter; and I must say that it does appear strange to me, that you should, on surmise, state such a thing of your commanding officer; but, Captain Wathen, as you have expressed a wish to enter into an explanation on the subject, I am ready to hear what you have to say." Captain Wathen then stated, that the amount of his troop debt had been created by an unusual supply of stable jackets, which had been sent to him from the tailor's shop, he did not know by whose orders, or for what purpose. My remark was, "Surely you must know that these jackets were sent to you by orders of your commanding officer; but has the supply of them been an unusual one?" Captain Wathen's reply was, "Yes, sir, I can prove it by my ledger, and the supply of them has created much discontent amongst the men of my troop." Addressing myself to Lieutenant-Colonel Lord Brudenell, I asked his lordship if the supply of the jackets was an unusual one? Lord Brudenell answered, "I can assure you, sir, the supply is not an unusual one, far from it; the men have not received near so many jackets within the last two years, as were issued to them before I assumed the command of the regiment." In addressing myself to Captain Wathen, I then said, "All this, sir, appears to me very extraordinary, but as you have stated that discontent was created amongst your men by the issue of the jackets in question, pray let me know if you have reported the circumstance to your commanding officer?" Captain Wathen replied, "Yes, sir, I did." On which Lord Brudenell, in a hasty manner, said, "I positively deny that Captain Wathen ever made such a report to me." In a tone of surprise I again repeated the question to Captain Wathen, and on his stating that he had made such a report to his commanding officer, Lord Brudenell said, "Sir, it is fal—." I immediately put up my hand, and said, "Lord Brudenell, stop"—and then requested Captain Wathen to withdraw. Shortly after Captain Wa-

Major-General Sir Thomas Arbuthnot's evidence.

Major-General Sir Thomas Arbuthnot's evidence.

then was requested to return, and I then sent for the quarter-master of the regiment, whom I questioned respecting the issue of the stable-jackets, asking him if the issue during the last two years was an unusual one? His reply was, "No, sir; when Colonel Thackwell commanded the regiment, an issue of full one-third was made to the men of the regiment in two years. Whereas the issue within the last two years up to the present period does not amount to one-sixth." It being then dark, I finished for that day my inspection of the 15th Hussars, stating to Lord Brudenell that as I had fixed the following day, Saturday, for the inspection of the 7th Dragoon Guards and Royal Artillery at Ballincollig, I would inspect the necessaries of the 15th on the Monday following, directing at the same time that the 15th should parade for that purpose in their stable-jackets. I forgot to mention that after I received an answer from the quarter-master respecting the relative issue of stable-jackets within the last two years up to this period and prior to it, I sent for all the commanding officers of troops, namely, Captains Rose, Macqueen, Ives, and Wood; to these officers, except Captain Wood, I put the question, if the late issue of jackets for the men of the troops under their command was an unusual one, and if such had created discontent amongst the men, the reply from each of them was in the negative. I then remarked; "Captain Wathen, it does appear to me extremely strange, that the men of your troop alone should be discontented on this subject;" having previously explained to the captains present, that Captain Wathen had said so, when to my surprise, Captain Wathen, in a very abrupt and disrespectful manner, as it appeared to me, said, "Sir, I did not say so,"—on which I remarked, "Surely, Captain Wathen, you cannot deny it;" and I appealed to Lord

Brudenell, my aide-de-camp, and the adjutant of the regiment, if you did not state that the issue of the jackets in question was an unusual one, and that such had created discontent amongst your men? They each of them replied positively in the affirmative. On this Captain Wathen remarked, "Really, sir, my mind was so irritated, and my feelings were such, that having yesterday been taunted by my commanding officer respecting the amount of my troop debt, that I may have said some things which I cannot *now* account for." Shortly after my arrival in the barrack-yard on Monday the 11th, I sent for Captain Wathen. Captain Wathen came; I requested that he would send for the serjeants of his troop, he having informed me on the Friday preceding that his serjeants had told him of the discontent of the men respecting the issue of the stable-jackets in question; on which Captain Wathen said, "General, you may recollect that I denied the other day that the serjeants had given me any such information. Pardon me, you must have misunderstood me." On which I said, "Captain Wathen, I could not have misunderstood you. You positively said so; and I appeal to Lord Brudenell and my aide-de-camp, if you did not say so;" both of whom positively said "Yes."

Major-General Sir Thomas Arbuthnot's evidence.

Subsequent to this, I went to the foot parade of the 15th to inspect their necessaries, &c.; these I found correct and good in all particulars, except in regard to the stable-jackets, many of which I examined were bad. Lord Brudenell brought me up the jacket of one particular man, and asked me if I thought it was in a fit state for a soldier to wear? My reply was, "Certainly not; a soldier of the 15th Hussars ought to be ashamed to wear such an old thing." Lord Brudenell then remarked, that he brought me up that particular jacket to prove that he paid due

Major-General Sir Thomas Arbuthnot's evidence.

attention to the interests of the soldiers in regard to the issue of new stable-jackets, for instead of ordering the man in question to have a new one, which would have cost him eighteen shillings, he had granted permission for the repair of the one in question, the doing of which would cost four or five shillings only. Then Lord Brudenell said, "You will be surprised that this man grumbles."

Q. Will you be so good as to state what was the state of the 15th Hussars at the inspection of the 8th of November.

[This question appearing objectionable to some of the members of the Court, the Court was cleared, and on its being re-opened, Lord Brudenell was informed that the Court had decided that the question should not be put.]

Witness wishes to add, that after Captain Wathen had stated to me on the 8th that the unusual issue of stable-ackets had caused the extent of the debt of his troop, and discontent amongst the men, which he had heard from his serjeants. I remarked, that if he had rested satisfied with stating that the unusual issue of jackets had in a great degree created the debt, I would have considered this in some degree a satisfactory explanation, but that I should have thought it my duty to point out to him as commanding officer of a troop, and to the commanding officer of the regiment, that when soldiers were likely to require articles of necessaries, of a costly nature, the men should, as authorized by the king's warrant, be placed under stoppages the month previous to that of issue. Captain Wathen's reply was, "Really, sir, I was induced to say what I did, in my own defence, in consequence of having been so frequently found fault with by Lord Brudenell. To this Lord Brudenell remarked, that till lately Captain Wathen's troop was in very bad order, and that he found it necessary to do so

Major-General Sir Thomas Arbuthnot's evidence.

Cross-examined by the prisoner.

Q. Did you, sir, at the inspection of the regiment, discover that my troop was in any way inferior either in the field or interior arrangements, to any other?

A. No; I did not.

Q. Did you, after the inspection was completed, observe that if any thing had been amiss, you must have discovered it?

A. I cannot recollect having made such observation, although such might have been likely, as I did not observe any difference between the troops.

Q. You have stated that you examined my books the last—How many officers had been in before me?

A. As far as I can recollect, three captains, Rose, Macqueen, and Ives.

Q. Did I not include cloth overalls as well as stable-jackets, when explaining to you the cause of the debt of my troop?

A. I think you did, and other articles of necessaries, to fit the men out for active service.

Q. At the time I pointed out the cause of my troop debt, did I not state to you, in presence of Lord Brudenell, that I did so in consequence of a previous discussion with his Lordship on the subject?

A. You did not, as far as I recollect, except in having mentioned, as already stated in my evidence, that you had been taunted by your commanding-officer, the day before, on the subject.

Q. Did you not say that I was right, at all events, in

Major-General Sir Thomas Arbuthnot's evidence.

in making the circumstance known to you, more particularly so, if there had been a previous discussion?

A. No.

Q. Did you put the question to Lord Brudenell whether there had been a previous conversation between his Lordship and myself on the subject of my troop debt?

A. I did not.

Q. Do you remember Lord Brudenell hesitating and faltering, and admitting that there had been a conversation between his Lordship and myself on the subject?

A. I really do not.

Q. Did I not take the earliest opportunity of removing from your mind the impression you seemed to entertain, that I intended to make a complaint against my commanding officer?

A. You did, by more than once saying that what you had stated respecting the issue of the stable-jackets, was in your own justification.

Q. Immediately upon understanding that you conceived I had said that my men had complained, and that I had heard so from my serjeants, did I not express my wish to remove that opinion from your mind?

A. No, you appeared to me to persevere in those assertions, till you denied them in the abrupt manner already alluded to, before the commanding-officers of troops.

Q. Did I not say that I had not mentioned the word complaint, but that *you* had asked me if complaints had been made to me by my men?

A. You did not make that remark to me, as far as I can recollect; but I asked you if any of the men had complained to you.

Q. In order to bring to your mind the circumstance of my not having said that the men complained, did I not ask you, at the time alluded to, if you did remember having asked me if the men complained, and that my reply was, "No, sir, they did not?"

Major-General Sir Thomas Arbuthnot's evidence.

A. When I asked you if the men had made complaints to you, you replied that they had not.

Q. Did not Lord Brudenell state some cause for the excess above the regulation, of my troop-debt, in the lists of debts and credits furnished by him to you?

A. In the return of debts of the regiment furnished to me by Lord Brudenell at the half-yearly inspection, he explained, opposite to the debts which exceeded 10*l*. of Cap. Wathen's, and I believe of two other troops, that such excess was caused by an issue of stable-jackets; and either in the return or in conversation, in consequence of the issue of other articles of necessaries to complete the men for service; and a remark was likewise made on the return, that, in his, Lord Brudenell's opinion, the issues in question should not have caused so large a debt as that which existed in Captain Wathen's troop. A further remark was made on this return, explaining that the stable-jackets in question, which had been inserted in Captain Wathen's ledger, had not been charged against the men of three other troops.

Q. Do you recollect the amount of debts of any other troops?

A. Yes: in Captain Rose's troop the debts amounted to 19*l*. 14*s*. 1¼*d*.; in Captain Macqueen's, 6*l*. 3*s*. 8*d*.; Captain Ives', 3*l*. 8*s*. 1¼*d*.; Captain Blythe's, 7*l*. 6*s*. 8*d*.; Captain Wood's, 16*l*. 19*s*. 3¼*d*. The foregoing statement is taken from the inspection return of debts.

Q. State to the Court the amount of debt of my troop?

A. 28*l*. 11*s*. 0¾*d*., as taken from the same document.

Q. Are you aware in which troops the jackets were not charged?

Major-General Sir Thomas Arbuthnot's evidence.

A. In Captain Macqueen's, Captain Ives', and Captain Blythe's troop, by the same document.

Q. Did Lord Brudenell explain why the jaokets were uot charged in the other troops?

A. He did not.

Q. Did you ever ask why the jackets were charged in my troop and not in the others?

A. I did not ask.

Q. Were the charges for stable-jackets inserted in Captains Rose's or Wood's troops, to your knowledge?

A. I am not aware that they were.

Tuesday, 24th Dec.—Cross-examination resumed.

Q. Did you inquire the cause of Captains Rose's and Wood's troop's debts being so much above the regulation, in which troops the stable-jackets, it appears, were not charged?

Document marked A.

A. By an explanation in a return of troop-debts now laid before the Court, and alluded to yesterday, signed by Lord Brudenell, it appears that 8*l.* of the debt in Captain Rose's troop belonged to one man, formerly a serjeant-major, who was reduced two years since. Opposite to Captain Wood's troop-debt it appears that the amount of this debt is to be attributed to the same causes remarked on in Captains Wathen's, Macqueen's, Ives', Blythe's, namely, to which troops the supply of stable-jackets and necessaries to complete them, when an order for embarkation was daily expected— having had this document before me before the inspection of the 15th Hussars was over, I did not make any particular inquiry why the stable-jackets had not been charged in the ledger, especially as Captains Rose and Ives informed me in the orderly-book that these entries had not been made, one or both of them explaining, that their men had notwithstanding been placed under stoppages for the payment of them.

Major-General Sir Thomas Arbuthnot's evidence.

Q. Were the whole of these remarks against these troops stated in the document when originally given to you, or added subsequently?

A. They were not all inserted in the first return which was handed to me; as far as I can recollect, those against Captain Wathen's troop were. I cannot speak in respect to the remark made opposite to Captain Rose's troop-debt, but having ascertained from some of the officers commanding troops, that the stable-jackets alluded to had not been charged in their ledger, I pointed out to Lieutenant-Colonel Lord Brudenell that it would be necessary for him to insert a remark to this effect, and I requested him to do so.

Q. What remarks were first in, and when was the present return given to you.

A. It will be seen by my last answer that I cannot speak with certainty as to the remarks which were inserted in the first return, which was first handed to me. I called for a return with the additional remarks, alluded to in my last answer, immediately after the officers commanding troops had left the regimental orderly room on the day of inspection, and I believe the return was sent to me on the same evening.

Q. Was it before or after I explained the cause of my troop-debt?

A. After.

Q. Did it not appear singular to you that the Lieutenant-Colonel should point out the debt of my troop in particular, and remark upon it, when his lordship was aware that the debts of other troops would have exceeded or equalled mine,

Major-General Sir Thomas Arbuthnot's evidence.

had not the charge of stable-jackets and overalls been withheld?

A. I must acknowledge that I did not ask Lord Brudenell if he was aware that the charges alluded to had not been inserted in the ledger of the troops commanded by other officers. I had no suspicion on my mind that a remark in this respect had been omitted intentionally, but having discovered the omission, I directed it should be rectified.

Q. Ought not Lord Brudenell to have included those troops in his remarks?

A. Most certainly, had he been aware that the entries alluded to had not been made in the ledgers.

Q. Did you ever inquire why he did not include those troops?

A I did not, further than the explanations which I have given in the foregoing answers.

Q. Was it not solely at your suggestion the remarks were made in the return?

A. It was.

Q. Was my explanation with regard to my troop-debt in any way the cause of the remarks being added to the returns?

A. It was, in addition to the avowals made by Captains Rose and Ives, stating that charges had not been entered in their ledger for the stable-jackets issued to the men.

Q. Did Lieutenant-Colonel Lord Brudenell ever state to you his reason why he ordered or admitted the charge for necessaries to be withheld in the accounts of some troops, and not in others?

A. Never, either directly or indirectly. I am not aware that such an order was ever given out by his Lordship.

Q. Ought he not to have done so?

A. Most certainly, under all the circumstances of the case, had such an order ever been given out.

Major-General Sir Thomas Arbuthnot's evidence.

Q. Ought he not to have done so if he was aware the charges were not made, although not by an order.

A. Certainly.

Q. When I stated the issues of stable-jackets and overalls to be the principal cause of my troop-debt, did I not designate it an unusual, and not that it was an unnecessary one?

A. You designated it as unusual.

Q. In reference to the issue of jackets and overalls, did I refer to the custom of other regiments than that to which I belonged?

A. You did not.

Q. Will you be good enough to state the nature of the conversation between yourself and Lord Brudenell when I was sent out of the office?

[Lord Brudenell objected to this question. The Court was cleared, and on its being re-opened, his Lordship was informed that the decision of the Court was that the question should be put.]

A. When Captain Wathen withdrew, I said, My Lord, you were, I fear, on the point of making use of a very objectionable expression to Captain Wathen; one which would have placed me in a very embarrassing situation, and I must request, that when I am addressing an officer, that you will not make any remarks, unless appealed to by me. Lord Brudenell bowed in a respectful manner, and Captain Wathen was then recalled.

Q. Do you recollect Lord Brudenell, in the conversation in the office, saying that the weekly mess-book would show what stoppages my troop was under for stable-jackets and cloth overalls?

Major-General Sir Thomas Arbuthnot's evidence.

A. I do not.

Q. Did he not ask your permission to send for this book?

A. I do not recollect his having done so.

Q. Did he not say he wished to show it to you, because what I had said about the number of men under stoppages was not the case?

A. I do not, in the slightest degree, recollect his lordship having said so, nor do I recollect your having said anything respecting your troop-debt, except in general terms.

Q. Did he not say, that so far from my having a great many men under stoppages, that there were so few, that he had sent for my serjeant-major to inquire why there were not more?

A. In speaking of Captain Wathen's troop-debt having been increased by the issue of the stable-jackets in question, Lord Brudenell informed me that sixty only, I think, had been issued to the whole regiment; of which a due proportion, namely, ten, had been sent to Captain Wathen's troop. I do not recollect Lord Brudenell having stated that he had sent for Captain Wathen's serjeant major, or that his Lordship, in the slightest degree, gave me to understand that the proper charges had not been brought against the men of that troop.

Q. From what period did you understand the issue of sixty jackets to allude, and were the overalls included?

A. From the time the last clothing was issued, which, to the end of this month, would be two years; the overalls were not included, as far as I can recollect.

Q. Did his Lordship show you the mess-book, when, shortly after, it was brought into the office?

A. He did not.

Q. In the interim between your having seen the regiment on Friday and finishing the inspection on the Monday following, did Lord Brudenell point to your notice the circumstance of my having given you a contradiction?

Major-General Sir Thomas Arbuthnot's Evidence.

A. I am not aware that he did so.

Q. Did he endeavour to put my conduct in a disadvantageous light?

A. Not that I am aware of. In the whole of this unpleasant affair I have acted completely upon my own judgment.

Q. After the inspection of the Infantry Depot had finished, on the 11th of November, did not your aide-de-camp take you aside from the assistant adjutant-general, and remind you of a circumstance relating to Captain Wathen?

A. He did not.

Q. Did you send for me on the 11th of November, and remind me of having given you a contradiction on the Friday previous?

A. On the 11th of November I sent for Capt. Wathen, and when he came I requested he would bring forward those serjeants who had informed him that the men of his troop were discontented at the issue of the stable-jackets in question. Captain Wathen then said "Sir, you may recollect that I denied the other day that the serjeants had given me such information, and that the men were discontented. Pardon me, General, you must have misunderstood me." My remark was, "Captain Wathen, I could not have misunderstood you; you certainly made the denial you mentioned the other day, and this, I must say, was done in a most improper and insubordinate manner."

Q. Did you notice that contradiction to me at the time it occurred?

A. I did, strongly commenting upon it, in the presence

Major-General Sir Thomas Arbuthnot's Evidence.

of Lord Brudenell, the Assistant Adjutant-General, my Aide-de-Camp, the Captains commanding troops assembled, the Adjutant, and I believe the Quarter-master.

Q. When you mentioned it to me on Monday, did you not qualify it by saying, you were quite sure I had not meant you offence, and that probably I was not aware of it myself.

A. On Captain Wathen's explanation, I expressed a hope and willingness to believe that he did not mean an offence to myself, remarking at the same time that I thought his conduct most extraordinary.

Q. Did you not say you had not liked to allude to it in the presence of the officers, but that certainly my contradiction was very flat?

A. Most positively not.

Q. Did you not say that on the former occasion, alluding to the Friday previous, you had pressed me hard upon some subject?

A. When Captain Wathen, on the 8th of November, informed me that discontents existed amongst some of his men respecting the issue of stable-jackets, I requested him to let me know how this came to his knowledge; he hesitated for some time in making a reply, when I pointed out to him that it was impossible for me to allow a matter of such a nature to remain without explanation; I said, "Captain Wathen, I must insist upon your telling me who gave you the information." He then stated his serjeants.

Q. Did I not say, it was natural my serjeant-major should point out to me the cause of my troop debt being so large?

A. Not that I recollect. Captain Wathen informed me when I had inspected his troop books that he settled his own accounts at the end of each month.

Q. From Lord Brudenell's subsequent representations, had you reason to believe that more than one of the men who complained during the two inspections belonged to my troop?

Major-General Sir Thomas Arbuthnot's Evidence.

A. At the time the men made the complaints alluded to, the 15th Hussars, both mounted and at the foot parade, was in column, and I do not know, nor ever did know, to what particular troop these men belonged; in fact, I paid no attention to that particular.

Q. May I request to know if it has been by your order that the second charge has been framed against me?

A. Not by my order, but the second charge was in two separate charges, and when shown to me by the assistant adjutant-general, I advised that they should be made into one charge, not, however, altering their substance.

Q. If Lord Brudenell had not preferred these charges, would you have done so?

A. Not without a reference to head-quarters.

Cross-examination finished.

Q. By the Court.—Did Captain Wathen appear in a state of excitement when the conversation took place between you and him on the 8th of November?

A. Not so at the commencement, but he did when all the officers commanding troops were assembled in the orderly-room by my direction.

Q. What was Captain Wathen's manner on the 11th, and state as nearly as you can what conversation passed on that day?

A. On Monday, the 11th, Captain Wathen appeared to me to be in a great state of excitement; his manner was proper and respectful. I have stated before what took place on that occasion.

Major-General Sir Thomas Arbuthnot's Evidence.

Q. When Liuetenant-Colonel Lord Brudenell made the observations to you regarding the private who grumbled about the charges for repairing his jacket, did his Lordship state the manner in which it had been done, or how he, Lord Brudenell, had heard of it?

A. He did not.

Q. Did it occur to you at the time, or do you now conceive that it might have referred to Captain Wathen's statement of the men of his troop being dissatisfied?

A. I conceived that the jacket was produced by Lord Brudenell to prove to me that he paid due attention to the interests of the soldiers under his command in allowing so old a jacket to be repaired instead of directing a new one to be issued, and this, I conceive, was in opposition to Captain Wathen's statement.

Q. You have stated, in answer to a question from the prisoner, that he, the prisoner, persevered in asserting that his men were dissatisfied; be pleased to state now the manner and time he so persevered in those assertions?

A. Captain Wathen informed me that he had understood from his serjeants that his men were dissatisfied at the issue of the stable-jackets in question; this he repeated on being questioned by me. I do not recollect having asserted that Captain Wathen otherwise persevered in asserting that his men were dissatisfied.

Q. Did Captain Wathen repeat the assertions of his men being dissatisfied at any other interview you had with him, except the one on Friday?

A. He did not.

Q. From any thing that has come to your knowledge as General of the district, either in writing or in conversation, relative to Lieutenant-Colonel Lord Brudenell and Captain Wathen, do you conceive that the former has in any instance been actuated by any inimical feeling towards the latter?

Major-General Sir Thomas Arbuthnot's Evidence.

A. I have cause to believe that Lord Brudenell's feelings towards Captain Wathen were not amicable.

Q. You have stated in a former answer the following: "If Lord Brudenell was aware the entries were not made in the ledgers." Is it possible his Lordship could be ignorant of the state of the ledgers at the period in question?

A. That depends upon the system of the 15th Hussars. In some regiments the ledgers are examined by a Board of officers, in others by the commanding officer himself. Under the former system a commanding officer may not every month know the exact state of the ledger, although the Board should report to him any irregularity of consequence they may discover.

Q. Did you ascertain from the serjeants or men of Captain Wathen's troop whether any discontent did exist respecting the issue of the stable-jackets, and if so whether the serjeants informed Captain Wathen of the existence of such discontent?

A. I did not address Captain Wathen's troop particularly on the subject, having put a question to the regiment in general including the subject.

Q. If you have no objection, pray state if you took any and what steps in consequence of Lord Brudenell's observation respecting the dissatisfaction expressed by the dragoon who objected to the sum charged for repairing his jacket.

A. I never understood that the man objected to the sum charged.

Q. Did you remark if the stable-jackets of Captain Wathen's troop were better or worse than those of the other troops of the 15th Hussars?

Major-General Sir Thomas Arbuthnot's Evidence.

A. I did not. I saw no difference.

Q. Did Lord Brudenell inform you how long these stable-jackets had been in wear, upon your perceiving they were in a bad state?

A. I understood from Lord Brudenell and the Quarter-master that the stable-jackets originally issued to the men were two years in wear, with the exception of the unexpired period to the end of this month.

Thursday, December 26th.

Q. By the Court.—Did it occur to you on ascertaining that Lieutenant-Colonel Lord Brudenell had made an observation in the inspection return now before the Court, on the debt of Captain Wathen's troop, and not on that of the others similarly circumstanced, that Captain Wathen had been correct in stating that he, Lord Brudenell, had made a complaint respecting the amount of debt of his troop, and that it was likely to cause him (Captain Wathen) to feel irritated when he first came before you, on the 8th of November?

A. This did not occur to me.

Q. Were you aware on the 8th of November that Lieut.-Colonel Lord Brudenell and Captain Wathen were not amicably disposed towards each other?

A. I had cause to believe this.

Q. Do you imagine this inimical feeling arose from points of duty, or otherwise?

A. As far as came to my knowledge, from points of duty only.

Q. Did you then or do you now conceive the feeling that subsisted between them to be of a nature that made them liable, when brought into collision, or placed in the situation they were on the 8th of November, to make use of any unguarded expressions?

Major-General Sir Thomas Arbuthnot's evidence.

A. I did then and do now.

Q. Do you conceive that Lieutenant-Colonel Lord Brudenell's having made use of the syllable fal—, might have been, in Captain Wathen's mind, tantamount to the full utterance of the word false—and the irritating feelings previously existing to be thereby aggravated?

A. I do.

Q. After Captain Wathen stated to you that his mind was so irritated, and his feelings being such at having been taunted by his commanding officer respecting the amount of his troop debt, that he might have said some things for which he could not account, did you give him an opportunity of explaining away any mis-statement?

A. I did, inasmuch as I was then, and on the 11th, ready and willing to pay attention to any explanation which Captain Wathen might have offered.

Q. Was any intimation made by you to Captain Wathen to that effect, and if so, in what manner?

A. None, that I can recollect.

Q. With reference to the latter part of the second charge, respecting Captain Wathen's repeating the denial of the statement he is said to have made to you on the 8th of November, do you not think that the repetition of the denial after what he had told you regarding the state of his mind, was to be expected as a matter of course?

A. My conclusion would be not.

Q. Did you or do you now ascribe Captain Wathen's manner, which you deemed insubordinate to the effects of excitement?

A. I did not then, but I do now.

Major-General Sir Thomas Arbuthnot's evidence.

Q. Do you imagine Captain Wathen made the statement to you wilfully, or that his irritated feelings may have caused the misrepresentation he made on the 8th, and which he was afterwards so anxious to correct?

A. Wilfully, actuated by his irritated feelings.

Q. When you say wilfully, do you wish the Court to understand that Captain Wathen's irritation induced him to make a representation, knowing it to be false?

A. Captain Wathen's statement in my estimation was wilful and decided; his irritated feelings may have bereft him of the power of reasoning on the subject at the time.

Q. Did you not consider the offensive word made use of in your presence by Lord Brudenell to Captain Wathen, coupled with anterior circumstances, sufficient to account for the excitement you observed in Captain Wathen?

A. Yes.

Q. Did you or do you now conceive the hasty manner which you have stated to have occurred on the part of Lieutenant-Colonel Lord Brudenell, together with the expression he used, to be equally insubordinate as that which occurred on the part of Captain Wathen?

A. I did not then, nor do I now.

Q. Did you ever explain or make known to Captain Wathen your disapproval of the offensive word and conduct of Lord Brudenell upon that occasion?

A. I never did.

Q. Is the Court to understand that you did not consider Lieutenant-Colonel Lord Brudenell's manner, and the expression he used, to be of an improper nature towards a junior officer?

A. The Court is not to understand that.

Q. If Captain Wathen had gone so far in expressing an

offensive syllable to any officer in your presence, would you not have required him to make immediate reparation, or have made him accountable for it?

Major-General Sir Thomas Arbuthnot's evidence.

A. Under all the circumstances of the case I would not have called on him to make immediate reparation, but I should have made him accountable for it.

Q. You have stated that " a remark was made in the return, stating that in his Lord Brudenell's opinion, the issues in question should not have caused so large a debt as that which existed in Captain Wathen's troop;" did his Lordship at any time inform you upon what grounds he formed that opinion?

A. Never.

Q. Be pleased to state, as nearly as you can, at what time of day on the 8th November you received the first return of debts of the 15th Hussars.

A. I conceive about three o'clock, after the inspection of the troop books.

Q. You have said that you cannot speak with certainty as to the remarks which were inserted in the first return of debts which was handed to you; be so good as to inform the Court whether you have that return, or whether you returned it to Lord Brudenell on calling for a more satisfactory one.

A. I have not that return, it was given back to Lord Brudenell.

Q. You have stated in your answer to a question in the prisoner's cross-examination, that when you asked Captain Wathen whether the men had made complaints to him, he replied that they had not; be so good as to explain the time when, and the place where, you put that question, and received that reply.

A. On the 8th of November, in the orderly-room.

Major-General Sir Thomas Arbuthnot's evidence.

Q. Are you aware why Lord Brudenell entertained feelings not amicable towards Captain Wathen?

A. Because when the decision of the general commanding-in-chief, on circumstances which took place in, as far as I can recollect, the month of September last, between Lieutenant-Colonel Lord Brudenell and Captain Wathen, was placed by me in his Lordship's hands to be read to Captain Wathen in the presence of the officers of the regiment, I requested that his Lordship, abiding by the decision of the general commanding-in-chief, would do every thing in his power to remove all bad feelings on the subject, when his Lordship told me, that after what had occurred, he could never be on terms of intimacy again with Captain Wathen.

Q. Did that conversation take place in Captain Wathen's presence?

A. It did not.

Q. Are you aware what steps were taken by Lieutenant-Colonel Lord Brudenell to remove the bad feelings alluded to?

A. I am not.

Q. Did you make any observation to Lieutenant-Colonel Lord Brudenell on his giving you the answer you have stated?

A. In general terms I combated the assertion, by giving the best advice in my power for the good of the service.

Q. Did you take any further steps to carry into effect the decision of the general commanding-in-chief?

A. I did not. At the time I spoke to Lord Brudenell, I remarked that no orders on my part could controul the mutual private feelings between officers; but that I was in hopes that time would wear away the feelings excited by what had occurred.

Q. Did you ever hear that Lord Brudenell added any

remarks of his own to the remarks of the general commanding-in-chief, when he communicated them to Captain Wathen? Major-General Sir Thomas Arbuthnot's evidence.

A. No.

Q. Do you imagine the inimical feelings of Lord Brudenell towards Captain Wathen were solely caused by the affair which called for the remarks of the general commanding-in-chief, which you gave to Lord Brudenell to read to the officers of the 15th Hussars?

A. As far as I can recollect, nothing came to my knowledge which could excite such feelings previous to the circumstances which took place in the month of September last.

Q. Did you recommend or assist in the formation of the other charges, and if so, particularize the charges you suggested or assisted in framing?

A. In the copy of the charges alluded to, shown to me by the assistant adjutant-general, in the first charge Captain Wathen was accused of having stated the old jackets would do; this I told Lord Brudenell I did not recollect, and that charge was altered accordingly. I did not give an opinion respecting the other charges. I beg leave to explain to the Court, that subsequently to this, Lieutenant-Colonel Lord Brudenell expressed a wish to consult me as the general officer commanding this district on points connected with the present trial; my reply was, that my situation was a very delicate one, as I was to be called upon as a witness, and no communication has consequently taken place between me and his Lordship on the subject. I also beg leave to explain to the Court, that I came to the same understanding with Colonel Turner, the assistant adjutant-general and my aide-de-camp, as they likewise are to be called upon as witnesses.

Major-General Sir Thomas Arbuthnot's evidence.

Q. Is the document now produced (marked letter B) the return of debts of the 15th Hussars, which was first handed to you by Lord Brudenell on the 8th of November, and is it in the same condition unaltered?

A. To the best of my knowledge it is, with the exception of the words "broken up" on the face of it.

Q. (*Through the Court by the prosecutor.*)—Did I not say that I would always treat Captain Wathen with perfect fairness, although I could not be on terms of intimacy with him?

A. You did on points of duty.

Q. Did I not tell you that I had always been on good terms with Captain Wathen, until he reported me to you in September last?

A. I cannot recollect such a circumstance.

Q. When I made use of the syllable "fal——" did I not instantly correct myself, and say, unfounded statement?

A. As far as I can recollect, yes.

Captain Charles Corkran's evidence.

Second witness for the Prosecution, Captain Charles Corkran, Aide-de-Camp to Major-General Sir Thomas Arbuthnot, was duly sworn, and examined on the three first charges by Lord Brudenell.

Q. With reference to the first charge, what did Captain Wathen state to Major-General Sir Thomas Arbuthnot, on the 8th of November last, relative to an unusual supply of new stable-jackets to the men of his troop?

A. Captain Wathen stated that an unusual number of stable-jackets had been issued to the men of his troop, he scarcely knew why or by whose authority?

Q. Did you hear me make any complaint of Captain

Wathen, or of his troop debt, or relative to his troop on any point? Captain Ch. Corkran's evidence.

A. No.

Q. Did you hear Captain Wathen say anything more respecting the issue of stable-jackets, except what you have stated?

A. He said that it created discontent amongst the men of his troop.

Friday, December 27th.

Q. (*By Prosecutor.*)—Did Captain Wathen tell the major-general how he was informed of this circumstance?

A. He said he had heard it from his serjeants.

Q. Did Captain Wathen say what course he had adopted on being informed by his serjeants that the men of his troop were discontented?

A. I cannot say positively.

Q. You have stated that Captain Wathen said that the issue of stable-jackets was unusual; did you hear him express any other opinion on the subject?

A. He said they were unnecessary.

Q. Do you recollect any particular expression being applied by Captain Wathen to Lord Brudenell's conduct?

A. Captain Wathen said that he had been taunted by Lord Brudenell.

Q. Upon what subject?

A. Upon the large amount of his troop debt.

Q. Did the major-general make particular inquiries of Captain Wathen relative to the alleged discontent of the men of Captain Wathen's troop?

A. Yes.

Q. What answer did Captain Wathen give?

Captain Ch. Corkran's evidence.

A. He attributed it to the unusual supply of stable-jackets.

Q. Were you, on the 8th of November 1833, ordered by Sir Thomas Arbuthnot to examine the inspection returns of the 15th Hussars?

A. Yes.

Q. Do you recollect whether, in the inspection return of troop debts, there were at that time any remarks entered by me in the column of remarks?

A. There were no remarks entered.

Q. Did the adjutant then ask you whether the remarks were to be entered by me, or the captains of troops?

A. Yes, he did.

Cross-examination by the Prisoner.

Q. When the major-general examined the books of the 15th Hussars, on the 8th of November, did he do so by seniority, and what officers preceded me?

A. You were the last troop officer whose books were examined.

Q. Were you not sitting at a side table and looking over the returns of debts and credits?

A. I was looking over all the returns during the time the general was examining the troop books.

Q. Did you not say, in reply to a question from the major-general, "Captain Wathen's debt is the greatest, it is twenty-eight pounds?"

A. When referred to by the general, I mentioned the amount of the debt.

Q. During the first conversation in the office, and with reference to my having said that the issue which had been, was unusual, did Lord Brudenell bring it to the notice of the major-general that I was making a complaint?

A. I cannot remember that he did. Captain Ch. Corkran's evidence.

Q. Did he, Lord Brudenell, say to the major-general, " Now, Sir, you allow him to go on in the same way you did the men in the field in the morning," or words to that effect?"

A. I don't remember it.

Q. Did he, Lord Brudenell, mention the word mutinous or mutiny?

A. Lord Brudenell interrupted Captain Wathen once or twice; but I don't remember his using either of those words.

Q. You say you don't remember; are you certain that the word or words were not used?

A. I am not certain that they were not used.

Q. Did the major-general intimate to Lord Brudenell to controul himself?

A. Yes, he did.

Q. Did I not, on my books being inspected, tell the major-general that the lieutenant-colonel had warned me on the previous day that I should have to account to him, the major-general, for the excess of my troop debt?

A. I think I remember your saying so.

Q. You said yesterday that I stated the jackets were issued I hardly knew by whose order; did I not state something of this sort in answer to a question put to me by the major-general, if they had been ordered without my knowledge?

A. I do not remember the general's question, nor your answer.

Q. In reference to a question the major-general put to Lord Brudenell, did his Lordship say, " No, I only said— I only said."

A. I do not remember these expressions being used.

Captain Ch. Corkran's evidence.

Q. When I was explaining to the major-general what I had meant to state, did I not say, "I intreat you, general, to call to mind the words I made use of?"

A. I do not recollect that you did.

Q. Was my manner respectful when explaining the misconception the major-general laboured under of the men having complained; and did I not more than once disavow having said that they had complained, or were discontented?

A. On one occasion I thought your manner abrupt. You did more than once disavow having said that the men of your troop were discontented.

Q. Did I mention to the major-general that Lord Brudenell was perpetually telling me that my troop was not only the worst in the regiment, but in the service?

A. I don't remember your using the word perpetually; but you told the general that Lord Brudenell had mentioned your troop as the worst in the regiment.

Q. Did not Lord Brudenell then say, addressing himself to me, "Well, Sir, is it not so?"

A. I don't recollect.

Q. What was the occasion of my leaving the office?

A. The general wished to speak to Lord Brudenell relative to an expression he had made use of.

Q. Do you not know or consider that the lieutenant-colonel entertained hostile feelings towards me?

A. I did not know anything upon the subject. My impression was that he was not friendly towards you.

Q. What was the expression made use of by the lieutenant-colonel before I was sent out of the office?

A. Lord Brudenell said that some statement which Captain Wathen had made was false.

Q. Did his Lordship say, "that some days ago, on looking at my weekly mess book, which showed the number of men under stoppages, he had observed there were so few, that he had sent for my serjeant, and asked him the reason?"

Captain Ch. Corkran's evidence.

A. I do not remember his having said so.

Q. Did you observe, on Monday the 11th, that I handed the major-general a return of jackets and overalls made up from my ledger?

A. No.

Q. When the major-general mentioned to me on Monday that I had contradicted him on Friday, (though he believed without meaning to offend,) did I not immediately apologize, and request him to be assured I did not intend to do so; and did he not appear to be satisfied with my apology?

A. Yes, you did, and I thought he appeared satisfied?

Q. Did you see the original debt and credit return?

A. Yes, I did; I conclude that that refers to the return I saw in the office.

Q. Can you identify the two returns now shown to you, marked A and B?

A. No, I won't undertake to identify them.

Cross-examination finished.

Q. By the Court.—With reference to the answer you gave to the prisoner's question, in saying, "I don't remember the general's question, or your answer," did you hear any question put by the major-general, and if so, state what it was, and the answer given by the prisoner?"

A. I do not remember any question being put.

Q. Did it appear to you that the general directed his attention to the debt in Captain Wathen's troop, more than

Captain Ch. Corkran's evidence.

to that of any other, and in every thing else relating to Captain Wathen's troop in the same manner?

A. Certainly not; his attention was called to the debt in Captain Wathen's troop by Captain Wathen himself.

Q. Were you, during the inspection of the 15th Hussars on the 8th November, and again on the 11th November, when that inspection was concluded, so near the person of the major-general, that you must have heard any questions addressed by him on points connected with that inspection?

A. Generally speaking, I was; sometimes I was sent away.

Q. As you have served in the cavalry, what time, in your opinion, should a stable-jacket last the dragoon?

A. About one year, I think.

Q. Did Sir Thomas Arbuthnot call for any explanation from Captain Wathen on the amount of his troop debt, or was Captain Wathen's explanation given voluntarily?

A. Captain Wathen's explanation was given voluntarily.

Q. Did you conceive Captain Wathen meant to make a report against his commanding officer, and thereby imputing improper conduct to him, when he, Captain Wathen, spoke to the major-general about the amount of the troop debt?

A. I certainly thought that it was an indirect accusation against his commanding officer.

Q. Was Captain Wathen in a state of excitement at the time?

A. Yes, I certainly thought he was.

Q. Did you see any thing invidious or improper in Captain Wathen's manner, when he stated to the major-general the cause why his troop was so much in debt?

A. No, not in the manner.

Captain Ch. Corkran's evidence.

Q. When Captain Wathen denied to the major-general having made the report stated in the second charge, do you conceive that his manner was improper and disrespectful, and if so, state in what respect?

A. I consider that his manner was disrespectful towards Sir Thomas Arbuthnot, on that occasion—it was abrupt.

Q. Do you conceive that manner to have been intentional, or to have arisen from irritated feelings?

A. I cannot think it was intentional; and if I remember right, Captain Wathen said at that moment, that his feelings were irritated.

Q. Do you imagine that Captain Wathen was so overcome by the irritation of his feelings, as to be rendered incapable of correctly judging whether he made a true or false report to the major-general.

A. I think he was capable of exercising his judgment.

Q. You said you were not certain whether the words "mutinous or mutiny" were made use of; could they have been without your hearing them?

A. They might have been made use of.

Q. Are you positive Lord Brudenell made use of the word false, as applied to Captain Wathen's statement?

A. Yes.

Q. Are you aware that it is the custom of the service to issue new stable-jackets to cavalry soldiers as they may require them, or is there any fixed time which such jackets are intended to last, and before the expiration of which period a fresh supply is not usually issued?

A. It is the custom of the service to issue new stable-jackets to cavalry soldiers as they are required.

Q. Do you speak positively as to its being a general custom, or do you confine it to the regiment in which you serve?

Captain Ch. Corkran's evidence.

A. I believe it to be the custom of all the cavalry regiments in our service.

Q. When you said that a stable-jacket was only calculated to last one year, did you speak of scarlet or blue jackets?

A. My experience was in scarlet jackets.

Colonel Ch. Turner's evidence.

Third witness for the Prosecution, Colonel Charles Turner, assistant adjutant-general of the southern district, was duly sworn and examined as to the first three charges.

Q. Please to state what occurred in the regimental office of the 15th Hussars, on the 8th November last, relative to Captain Wathen.

A. I heard Major-General Sir Thomas Arbuthnot address Captain Wathen, that it was extraordinary that the men of his troop alone should have been discontented with the issue of stable-jackets, on which Captain Wathen denied in an abrupt manner that the men were discontented. Sir Thomas Arbuthnot afterwards repeated, in the presence of captains of troops assembled in the orderly-room, that Captain Wathen had stated to him, Sir Thomas Arbuthnot, that the serjeant had informed him, Captain Wathen, that the men had expressed discontent, on which Captain Wathen said, "I really felt so hurt and irritated at what had occurred the day before in the orderly-room, on the subject of my troop debt, having been so taunted by Lord Brudenell, that I really cannot account for what I may have said," or words to that effect.

Q. Did you consider Captain Wathen's manner disrespectful, when he denied that his men were discontented on that occasion?

A. By the abrupt manner in which he denied the statement, and without that qualification which followed, I must say, I did consider his manner disrespectful.

Colonel Ch. Turner's evidence.

Q. Did not Captain Wathen, at the time to which you refer, state positively to Major-General Sir Thomas Arbuthnot, that he had not mentioned to him, Sir Thomas Arbuthnot, at an earlier hour in the day, that the serjeant had reported to him, Captain Wathen, that the men of his troop had expressed discontent?

A. I cannot speak positively.

Q. Did the captains of troops, when addressed by Sir Thomas Arbuthnot, say that the men of their troops were discontented at the issue of new stable-jackets, or did they say that an unusual issue of stable-jackets had taken place in their troops?

A. In neither case did they admit that there had been discontent in their troops, or an unusual issue of stable-jackets.

Q. What did Sir Thomas Arbuthnot say to Captain Wathen previous to the parade of the 15th Hussars, on Monday, the 11th November last.

A. Major-General Sir Thomas Arbuthnot requested Captain Wathen would bring forward the serjeant who gave him the information that discontent prevailed in his troop at the issue of these new stable-jackets, on which Captain Wathen said, "I beg to remind you that I denied the other day that discontent existed in my troop; pardon me for saying so, Sir, you must have misunderstood me."

Q. What reply did the major-general then make to Captain Wathen?

A. "I could not have been mistaken;" and he appealed to Lord Brudenell and his aide-de-camp on the subject, who agreed with him.

Q. Are you quite sure that Captain Wathen said serjeant?

Colonel Ch. Turner's evidence.

A. I cannot be positive.

Q. Do you know any thing of what occurred in the regimental office of the 15th Hussars, on the 8th of November last, at an earlier hour than that to which you have already alluded, between Sir Thomas Arbuthnot and Captain Wathen?

A. Nothing.

Cross-examined by the Prisoner.

Q. You have stated that I replied in an abrupt manner to the major-general; did I not appear to you to have been agitated and excited from some previous discussion?

A. Very much so indeed.

Q. In the regimental-office on the 8th of November, did the major-general tell me my conduct was insubordinate or improper, in contradicting him?

A. I do not recollect that he made use of the word insubordinate, but Sir Thomas was much displeased with the manner you had replied to him, and also for having made use of the word "taunted," towards your commanding officer.

Q. Did I not on Monday apologize for any unintentional contradiction I might have given to the major-general on Friday, and was he not apparently satisfied with it?

A. You did endeavour to explain away the contradiction which occurred on the 8th, but whether Sir Thomas Arbuthnot was satisfied, or considered that sufficient, I cannot say; Captain Wathen expressed himself in a most quiet gentleman-like manner.

Q. You have said that the troop officers said that their men were not discontented at the issue of stable-jackets; are you aware whether their men had been charged for them in their accounts?

A. I have heard one or two of the captains, on their return to the office, say that it was right to inform Sir Thomas Arbuthnot that the men of their troop had not been charged for new stable-jackets. Colonel Ch. Turner's evidence.

Q. Do you consider Lord Brudenell to be actuated in bringing forward the present charges, by a desire to promote the good of the service, or from any other motives?

A. I cannot suppose his Lordship could have been actuated by any other cause than that of discipline of the service.

Saturday, December 28.—*Cross-examination resumed.*

Q. Do you suppose I willingly or knowingly gave the major-general cause of offence?

A. I cannot suppose you did.

Q. Do you consider that Lord Brudenell was not amicably disposed towards me?

A. I cannot say.

Q. Do you remember my presenting a paper or return to the major-general on the afternoon of the 11th of November, when he first sent for me?

A. I cannot call that circumstance to my recollection.

Q. Do you remember my saying to the major-general, "Here is a return of jackets and overalls, made up from my ledger?"

A. I cannot speak positively, but I think I have a recollection of your saying so.

Q. Was it not at your intercession that I was allowed to walk at any time in the barrack-yard, without confining myself to two hours' exercise?

A. I did write to Lord Brudenell to express the major-general's hope that the same indulgence was granted to

Colonel Ch. Turner's evidence.

Captain Wathen to take exercise as upon a former occasion.

Q. By the Court. Did you hear the major-general ask the 15th Hussars on parade if they had any complaints, and if so, did any of the men come forward?

A. I did hear the major-general ask the 15th Hussars if they had any complaints, and I think three men came forward with complaints, totally unconnected with the present charges.

Q. Did you conceive Captain Wathen meant to make a report against his commanding officer, and thereby imputing improper conduct to him, when he Captain Wathen spoke to the major-general about the amount of his troop debt?

A. I cannot say; I was not present at the time alluded to.

Q. Were you present at any time, on the 8th or 11th of November, when Captain Wathen was in a state of excitement.

A. I was present in the orderly-room of the 15th Hussars, on the afternoon of the 8th of November, when he appeared very much excited.

Q. Do you imagine that Captain Wathen was so overcome by the irritation of his feelings, as to be rendered incapable of correctly judging whether he made a true or false report to the major-general?

A. I think he never would have made so abrupt and flat denial to the major-general, had his mind been in a more composed state.

Q. Do you consider the conduct of Captain Wathen, at any time during the inspection of the 15th Hussars, to have been unbecoming the character of an officer and a gentleman?

A. As regards the denial, he forgot himself as a gentleman. Colonel Ch. Turner's evidence.

Q. Have you seen the lists of debts and credits of the 15th Hussars, presented to the major-general on the 8th of November?

A. I had, I presume, in my possession that document, which was sent by the major-general, with various other papers, to me about a week ago. I read the purport of it on the back of the return, but never opened it, and which return was called for by the major-general on the second day of his examination, which I gave to Captain Corkran to be handed into court.

Q. Did you at any time during the inspection of the 15th Hussars, observe any thing irritating or domineering in the manner of Lord Brudenell towards Captain Wathen, either when addressing that officer or speaking of him?

A. No, I did not.

Q. *(By the Prosecutor, through the Court.)*—What answer did Lord Brudenell write to your communication relative to Captain Wathen having the liberty of taking exercise in the barrack-yard?

A. That he had full permission, without restriction, to take such exercise as he pleased for the benefit of his health.

Q. *(By the Court.)*—Are you aware what the restrictions were which Captain Wathen was under that caused your letter to Lord Brudenell, and if so, state them?

A. I am not aware that there were any restrictions; but the cause of my writing to Lord Brudenell was in consequence of a paragraph having appeared in one of the Cork papers, stating that Captain Wathen was prevented taking exercise which his health required, or words to that effect.

Colonel Ch. Turner's evidence.

Q. (*By Lord Brudenell, through the Court.*)—Did not Lord Brudenell rather say in his private note to which you allude, that no restrictions had been recently imposed on Captain Wathen taking exercise in the barrack-yard; that I had seen him out on that day, and believed he took exercise every day?

A. Yes, those were the expressions made use of.

Q. (*By the Court.*)—When was Captain Wathen placed in arrest; and when did you write to Lord Brudenell as alluded to?

A. Captain Wathen was placed in arrest on the 12th of November, and reported to me on the 13th; and I wrote to Lord Brudenell on the 11th of December.

Lieutenant C. Higginson Jansh Hecker's evidence.

Fourth witness for the Prosecution, Lieutenant C. Higginson Jansh Hecker, lieutenant and adjutant of the 15th Hussars.

Q. With reference to the first charge, what did Captain Wathen say on the 8th of November last to Major-General Sir Thomas Arbuthnot, about an unusual supply of stable-jackets to his men?

A. On the 8th of November I was in the regimental office, in my capacity as adjutant of the regiment, at the time Major-General Sir Thomas Arbuthnot inspected the troop books of Captain Wathen's troop. The major-general had inspected the whole of the books belonging to Captain Wathen's troop, and had made his remarks thereon, when Captain Wathen commenced voluntarily to give an explanation why his troop debt was so large; stating that an unusual number of stable-jackets had been issued out to the men of his troop which he had charged in his troop ledger.

Q. What else did he state on the subject with reference to the first charge?

A. Captain Wathen further stated, that he was not aware of the said jackets being given out to the men of his troop.

Lieutenant C. Higginson Jansh Hecker's evidence.

Q. Did he say anything about his men, with reference to the second charge?

A. With reference to the second charge, Captain Wathen said, that the men of his troop receiving the said jackets were discontented; and upon being further questioned by the major-general, from whom he had heard that the men were discontented, he stated that he had heard it through the serjeants of his troop.

Q. With rererence to the third charge, did Captain Wathen say what course he adopted when the serjeants reported to him that the men were discontented?

A. Captain Wathen said that he had mentioned to Lord Brudenell, that he had heard that there was discontent amongst the men of his troop on the subject of the above issue of stable-jackets.

Q. When Captain Wathen had made the above statements, had I made any complaint about his troop debt or his troop to Major-General Sir Thomas Arbuthnot?

A. Not to my knowledge.

Q. Did Captain Wathen repeat his statement to the major-general that the serjeants had reported to him that the men were discontented at the issue of new stable-jackets, and that he had mentioned the circumstance to me?

A. I have no recollection of the repetition of either one assertion or the other.

Q. Had I applied any harsh term to Captain Wathen previous to his making the above statements, or had I said any thing calculated to irritate him?

A. On the 8th of November I heard no harsh words ap-

Lieutenant C. Higginson Jansh Hecker's evidence.

plied to Captain Wathen by Lord Brudenell. On the morning before the inspection of the 8th of November there was a conversation in the regimental office between Captain Wathen and Lord Brudenell, respecting the excess of his troop debt. Captain Wathen was asked by Lord Brudenell the reason why his troop debt was so large? Captain Wathen stated, in reply, that numerous articles had been issued out to the men of his troop, which had been entered on his ledger, and had increased the amount of his debt. Reference was then made by Lord Brudenell to the debt of another troop, which was considerably lower than Captain Wathen's. Captain Wathen answered, that he was responsible only for his own debt, and that, perhaps, the troop debt to which allusion was made was small, in consequence of the articles which had been issued out to that troop not being charged in the ledger.

Q. Did I speak harshly to him on that occasion, or in the shape of a reprimand?

A. No, I did not consider it so.

Q. You have stated that Captain Wathen told the major-general that the issue of stable-jackets was unusual; did he say that it was any thing else?

A. I have no recollection of his having done so.

Q. Do you recollect Captain Wathen being ordered by the major-general to leave the regimental office?

A. I do.

Q. Was it previous to this circumstance that Captain Wathen had made statements relative to the discontent of his men, and of his having mentioned the circumstance to Lieutenant-Colonel Lord Brudenell?

A. To the best of my recollection it was subsequent.

Q. Were you in the regimental office when Captain Wathen was ordered to withdraw?

Lieutenant C. Higginson Teush Hecker's evidence.

A. I was, on one occasion.

Q. What was the cause of Captain Wathen's being ordered to withdraw?

A. It followed immediately upon Lord Brudenell's denial to the major-general, that Captain Wathen had mentioned to him (Lord Brudenell) that he had heard there was discontent amongst the men of his troop, on the subject of the stable-jackets.

Q. Do you know how many stable-jackets were charged in Captain Wathen's troop ledger previous to the day of inspection?

A. From my own personal inspection of Captain Wathen's ledger I could only find nine.

Q. Be so good as to state the mode in which I rejected the bad stable-jackets in Captain Wathen's troop and the regiment?

A. At all dismounted parades the regiment was generally inspected by Lord Brudenell, in open column of troops; the ranks were opened by the officers commanding the troop for Lord Brudenell's inspection of the rank. Lord Brudenell was followed down the ranks by the officer commanding the troop and by myself; if any jacket appeared to Lord Brudenell either to require repairs, or that the man should have a new one, it was pointed out to the officer commanding the troop, who received orders that the jacket should be shown in the regimental office for Lord Brudenell's further inspection and decision.

Q. In what manner were those jackets which had been pointed out on parade, again inspected by me; and who was present on those occasions in the office?

A. The names of those men, to whom the jackets belonged, were given to the senior non-commissioned officer, by the officer commanding the troop on the parade above

Lieutenant C. Higginson Teush Hecker's evidence.

alluded to. The next day, or some days, might intervene, (other duties interfering.) The men, accompanied by a non-commissioned officer, and, generally speaking by the serjeant-major of the troop, were ordered to come themselves with their jackets in their hands, their regimental quarter-master, and the regimental master tailor were ordered on the occasion to be present. Lord Brudenell, after having inspected the jacket, again himself, called upon the regimental quarter-master for his opinion as to the possibility of its being repaired, so as to be fit to come to parade; in the event of the regimental quarter-master giving it as his opinion that, with certain repairs, the jacket could be made fit for parade, the regimental master-tailor was asked what the cost to the man would be to put it into the required repair, the man was told what the charge to him would be, and was then questioned whether he would prefer paying for the repairs of the old jacket, or have a new one.

Q. Did the men often express dissatisfaction on those occasions at having to purchase new jackets?

A. No, generally speaking they preferred paying for the new jackets to having the old one repaired.

Q. Were any stable-jackets rejected in any other manner except by my own personal inspection and decision?

A. Not to my knowledge.

Q. With reference to the interview, which you have stated to have taken place between Captain Wathen and myself, the day previous to the day of inspection, what expression did Captain Wathen report to the major-general that I had applied to him with reference to his troop debt?

A. Captain Wathen said that Lord Brudenell had taunted him with his troop debt.

Q. You have said that Captain Wathen was ordered to leave the office on the 8th of November, in consequence of a denial which Lord Brudenell had made to Captain Wathen, of the latter having mentioned to him, Lord Brudenell, that his men were discontented. Do you recollect the word which Lord Brudenell made use of on that occasion? Lieutenant C. Higginson TeushHecker's evidence.

A. I cannot positively say.

Q. When Major-General Sir Thomas Arbuthnot came to the regimental office of the 15th Hussars on the 8th of November last, had any remarks been inserted by me in the return of troop debts?

A. No.

Q. When were the inspection returns sent off to the assistant adjutant-general's office?

A. To the best of my recollection, it was on Sunday, the 10th.

Cross-examination by the Prisoner.

Q. Since my release from former arrest by order of Lord Hill, has the lieutenant-colonel often found fault with me and my troop?

A. Yes.

Q. Did you at any time hear any harsh remark applied to me by Lord Brudenell?

A. On no other occasion, that I can recollect, except once in the drill-field.

Q. State what it was?

A. It was at a field day, a short time previous to the inspection, when Captain Wathen was told by Lord Brudenell that a junior officer should be put in command of his troop.

Lieutenant C. Higginson Teush Hecker's evidence.

Q Do you remember coming to me at stable-time after a field day, on the 4th of November last, and saying, "The colonel wants you and Surret in the office directly; he is to come as he is, in his stable-jacket, without waiting?"

A. Perfectly so.

Q. Previous to your coming to call private Surret and myself into the office, had you any conversation with Lord Brudenell, as to what might take place?

A. To the best of my recollection, none whatever.

Q. Had you been directed to take down in writing what I should say?

A. I had been long previously told by Lord Brudenell to commit to writing the nature of what occurred in the regimental office.

Q. With what view was it that my words were to be taken down?

A. I have no means of saying; I merely acted from the orders I had received from Lord Brudenell.

Q. Did private Surret, when in the office, decline to sign his accounts?

A. Yes, he did.

Q. Did Lord Brudenell find fault with any troop in private Surret's presence?

A. Yes, he did.

Q. Did I, while the private remained in the office, make any remarks on what the lieutenant-colonel had said?

A. To the best of my recollection, not.

Q. Did I speak to him on the subject after the private left the office?

A. You did.

Q. After I withdrew, was I shortly afterwards recalled,

and did not the lieutenant-colonel then show me a paper, on which he said my words were written down, and ask whether I could deny them?

Lieutenant C. Higginson TeushHecker's evidence.

A. Captain Wathen was shortly afterwards recalled, and the paper, to which Captain Wathen alludes, was by Lieutenant-Colonel Lord Brudenell shown to Captain Wathen, but I have no recollection of Lord Brudenell asking Captain Wathen if he could deny them.

Q. How long has it been established in the king's Hussars that conversations between the commanding officers and the officers in the orderly room should be committed to writing by you?

A. In answer to the first part of the question, I cannot say how long it has been established in the regiment, but can state that I received the order from Lord Brudenell, immediately after my being appointed adjutant to the regiment, the 17th of August, 1832, to commit to paper the nature of conversations which might occur in the regimental office.

Q. Have the officers been warned, or made acquainted, before they entered into conversation with the lieutenant-colonel, that you were so employed?

A. They were not so warned by me.

Q. You have stated that you noted down what occurred in the regimental office, in consequence of general instructions for that purpose long previously given by Lord Brudenell; do you mean to say that you received no instructions from his Lordship to note down in particular what occurred between his Lordship and myself?

A. None.

Q. On the day previous to the inspection, when I explained to Lord Brudenell the cause of my troop debt,

Lieutenant C. Higginson TeushHecker's evidence.

did his Lordship say that my reasons were not sufficient, that it was my bad management?

A. Lord Brudenell did say, that he did not consider Captain Wathen's explanation of the excess of his troop debt sufficient, but I do not recollect Lord Brudenell's attributing it to bad management on the part of Captain Wathen.

Q. When you said that Lord Brudenell made no remarks in the debt and credit lists, did you allude to the returns of the troop officers, or to the regimental return?

A. To the regimental return.

Q. Who ordered the addition to the original debt and credit return?

A. Lord Brudenell put in the remarks himself.

Q. After the inspection, what was the reason I was not called into the office in my turn to have my books examined?

A. I have no recollection of the reason why he was not called in in his turn.

Q. Did Lord Brudenell, when making denial of what I was said to have stated to Major-general Sir Thomas Arbuthnot, say it was false?

A. I did not hear Lord Brudenell make use of that word.

Q. With reference to my having explained the cause of my troop debt, did the major-general say, "O, if there has been a previous discussion, Captain Wathen is quite right; I consider him right, at all events, in bringing the circumstance to my notice," or some such words?

A. I do not recollect the major-general saying so, or using words to that effect.

Q. Did the lieutenant-colonel say to the major-general, without reference to what I had said about the jackets and overalls, that I was making complaints?

A. To the best of my recollection, he did.

Lieutenant C. Higginson Teush Hecker's evidence.

Q. During the conversation in the regimental-office, was the word mutiny or mutinous made use of?

A. I heard neither one word or the other used.

Q. Did the major-general intimate to Lord Brudenell to controul himself?

A. The major-general did make a sign to Lord Brudenell, which appeared to me to convey a wish that Lord Brudenell should allow him, the major-general, to hear the whole matter explained without interruption.

Q. Have you seen the evidence which has been given by the major-general, or Captain Corkran, or has it been made known to you either directly or indirectly?

A. No, neither.

Q. By the Court. When you heard Captain Wathen voluntarily give an explanation to Major-General Sir Thomas Arbuthnot, why his troop debt was so large, were you in a situation at the time to hear every thing that passed between Sir Thomas and him?

A. I was.

Q. Did you hear Sir Thomas Arbuthnot desire Captain Wathen to make any statement in the way of explanation on that occasion; and if so, state what it was?

A. The major-general did desire Captain Wathen to give what explanation he thought proper.

Q. Do you think it possible that the syllable fal ——, or the word false, could have been used without your hearing it in the regimental office at the time alluded to?

A. I think it possible the syllable fal—— might have been made use of, but I feel persuaded that if the word false had been made use of, I should have heard it.

Q. When the conversation took place between Lord Brudenell and Captain Wathen in the regimental office on the morning before the 8th of November, did Lord Bru-

Lieutenant C. Higginson TeushHecker's evidence.

denell express himself to Captain Wathen in his ordinary tone of voice and manner, while speaking to the officers of the 15th Hussars?

A. Lord Brudenell's voice was raised above the ordinary tone.

Q. For what purpose was private Surret so suddenly called to appear before Lieutenant-Colonel Lord Brudenell?

A. In order that Lord Brudenell might ascertain from him the reason why he refused to sign his accounts.

Q. Is it the usual manner in the 15th Hussars of calling the men before the commanding officer?

A. Yes.

Q. Why did private Surret refuse to sign his accounts?

A. On account of having the marks of disgrace put on his arm.

Q. Is it an established system in the 15th Hussars, that the quarter-master decides whether a soldier's jacket is fit to be repaired or a new one being necessary?

A. I am not aware that it is the established system.

Q. How did it so happen on the occasion you have mentioned?

A. It has been customary lately, since Lord Brudenell's command of the regiment?

Q. What had occurred in the drill-field to make Lord Brudenell tell Captain Wathen that a junior officer should be put in command of his troop?

A. On the occasion of the regiment trotting past in open column of troop, Captain Wathen placed himself in the front of the centre of his troop, on the troop arriving on the passing line, and trotted past in that position?

Q. Did Lord Brudenell make the observation in full hearing of the men?

A. He did. Lieutenant C. Higginson TeushHecker's evidence.

Q. Had any other officer made at any time a similar mistake without the same notice being taken of it?

A. I have a recollection of the same mistake being made, and on some occasions Lord Brudenell has remarked it and spoken to the officer, but not, I think, to the same extent as Captain Wathen was spoken to.

Q. Are you aware of any other reason for Lord Brudenell's telling Captain Wathen he would put another officer to command his troop, but the mistake he, Captain Wathen, made on the occasion you mention?

A. I consider that Lord Brudenell said that he would put a junior officer to command the troop, solely on account of the mistake Captain Wathen had made.

Q. Do you not conceive an officer may make the mistake very easily, the place of an officer, when trotting past, being so recently changed by the new regulations.

A. The regiment had had such frequent practice in the new cavalry regulations, that I consider almost every officer in the regiment must be acquainted with the change therein made.

Q. Do you then consider Captain Wathen's mistake to have been wilful?

A. Certainly not.

Q. How long had Captain Wathen been released from his former arrest, when Lord Brudenell said he would put a junior officer in command of his troop?

A. Captain Wathen was released from arrest the 20th of October, and the circumstance alluded to occurred a few days before the inspection on the 8th of November.

Q. How long had Captain Wathen been under the first arrest?

A. From the 25th of September to the 20th of October.

Lieutenant C. Higginson TeushHecker's evidence.

Q. State to the Court your daily duties as adjutant of the 15th Hussars, since the first of November last.

A. There have been three field days a-week, at which I attended; on two of the intermediate days of the week I have taken out a squadron of the regiment, mounted, for the purpose of skirmishing drill; on the Saturday there has usually been a watering parade at which all officers attended; on Sunday the troops are paraded for divine service, at which all officers are present, and accompany the troops to church. Upon those days upon which the troops went to the field for the purpose of field exercise, the orderly time was, in consequence of the troops being out at exercise, put off later than eleven o'clock, which hour is the hour named in the standing orders of the regiment, that all business connected with the regimental-office should commence: on the other occasions, when the troops did not go to the field, the orderly time did commence, generally speaking, at eleven o'clock; the period at which the business of the regimental office would finish, of course depended on the business then to be done.

Q. Do the officers attend the skirmishing drill, and do you drill the men and officers on foot parade?

A. Some of the junior officers do attend the skirmishing drills, and the same junior officers have latterly been drilled by me on foot parade in the afternoon with the men.

Q. Have you been in the habit of going through the regimental stables?

A. I have nearly always accompanied the commanding officer round the stables when he went; at no other time am I required; I have occasionally gone round the stables by myself.

Q. Have you observed any difference in the condition or grooming of the horses in Captain Wathen's troop to those of the other troops? Lieutenant C. Higginson Teush Hecker's evidence.

A. I have observed a difference in the condition and grooming of Captain Wathen's troop, as far as regards some of the horses.

Q. State the number of horses, and to what cause you ascribed the difference?

A. There were about half a dozen horses in Captain Wathen's troop whose condition was low, but not more so than I have usually known them to be; their coats were long; the above-named horses I have always known to have been in the aforesaid low condition, as they are naturally so.

Q. Have you not observed a difference in the condition and grooming in some horses of other troops?

A. Yes.

Q. State how many.

A. I should think the average to be about three or four in the other troops.

Q. Have more irregularities occurred in Captain Wathen's troop, on the part of the non-commissioned officers and men, than in any other troop? and if so, state them.

A. I think that latterly the list of defaulters has been heavier in Captain Wathen's troop than in the other troops, although not to any great extent.

Q. State the nature of them, and to what cause you ascribe them.

A. There have been, generally speaking, cases of absence from roll-call, and some cases of drunkenness; the only cause to which I can ascribe them is the circumstance of the soldier's pay allowing him to procure for the same sum more liquor in this country than he could do in England.

Lieutenant C. Higginson TeushHecker's evidence.

Q. Have you had any conversations with Lord Brudenell since the 1st of November last relative to Captain Wathen individually, or to his troop? and if so, state the time they took place, and what passed on each occasion.

A. On the return of the troops from the field on the day to which I have already alluded, when Captain Wathen was spoken to by Lord Brudenell in the field, Lord Brudenell did speak to me on the subject of Captain Wathen, and said, that it was quite inconceivable how Captain Wathen could have made the mistake he did on that day. To the best of my recollection, on the morning of the inspection, Lord Brudenell did ask me whether I thought Captain Wathen would commit any mistake similar to the one he had already committed upon the occasion above alluded to. I said, I did not think that he would. I have no recollection of any other.

Q. Are you on good terms with Captain Wathen?

A. Yes, to my knowledge; during Captain Wathen's arrest, I thought it my duty to hold as little communication with him as possible.

Q. Has Captain Wathen been in the habit of making mistakes in the field when the regiment has been at drill under Lord Brudenell?

A. Perhaps not more frequently so than some other officers.

Q. When did you first see the inspection return of troop debts now produced to you, marked letter A?

A. On the 8th of November.

Q. Were the observations thereon stated when you first saw it?

A. No; it contained no observations, but the amount of the debt.

Q. What caused the observations being made?

Lieutenant C. Higginson TeushHecker's evidence.

A. I had ascertained from Captain Corkran, aide-de-camp to the major-general, that the remarks were to be put in by Lord Brudenell.

Q. Did you at any time see the return with the remarks relative to Captain Wathen's troop stated, without referring to any of the others?

A. I did not.

Q. Did Captain Corkran specify the remarks to be inserted by Lord Brudenell?

A. Not to me.

Q. Were the stable-jackets of Captain Wathen's troop generally in a better or worse state than the other troops of the 15th Hussars?

A. I never observed that they were better or worse than those of any other troop.

Q. Can you state if the excess of the debt of 18*l.* 11*s.* $0\frac{3}{4}$*d.* above the usual regulations, was occasioned in Captain Wathen's troop by a supply of stable-jackets and overalls issued to that troop?

A. I should think, in a great measure, it must be so.

Q. Do you know to what period were the accounts closed in the ledgers that were submitted to Major-General Sir Thomas Arbuthnot's inspection on the 8th of November?

A. Up to the end of the preceding month.

Q. Is it not usual, in the 15th Hussars, to charge every article of necessaries in the ledger when they are received by the dragoon?

A. It is usual.

Q. Is it the custom, in the 15th Hussars, to issue articles of clothing or necessaries to the troops, without the knowledge of the officers commanding troops?

A. Clothing has been issued without the immediate

Lieutenant C. Higginson TeushHecker's evidence.

knowledge perhaps of the officer commanding the troop, but all articles of regimental necessaries not.

Q. Have you any means of knowing why the stable-jackets issued to the Hussars of the other troops were not charged against them as those of Captain Wathen's were?

A. None.

Q. What is the system in the 15th Hussars relative to the examination of the troop ledgers for the information of the commanding officer?

A. Lord Brudenell has either inspected the troop ledgers himself, or has ordered the senior major of the regiment to do so, and report thereon to him.

Q. Did you hear Captain Wathen, when his books were examined, tell Major-General Sir Thomas Arbuthnot, that Lieutenant-Colonel Lord Brudenell had warned him on the previous day that he should have to account to him, the major-general, for the excess of his troop debt?

A. I do not recollect his having done so.

Q. You have stated the word "false" could not have been made use of by Lord Brudenell in the orderly-room without your knowledge; was the syllable "fal—," or any word or syllable used by his Lordship towards Captain Wathen, which went to accuse him of making a statement unfounded in fact; and if so, what word or syllable was used by Lord Brudenell?

A. I did not hear the syllable "fal—" used, but to the best of my recollection, Lord Brudenell did say that the statement was unfounded.

Q. You have stated that you received general directions from Lord Brudenell to commit to writing every conversation that might take place in the orderly-room; will you be pleased to state to the Court the time when you took down the last conversation that happened in the orderly-room previous to November the 4th, and with whom?

Lieutenant C. Higginson TeushHecker's evidence.

A. I committed to writing the nature of a conversation which occurred in the orderly-room between Lord Brudenell and Lieutenant Naylor of the 15th Hussars, previous to the 4th of November.

Q. State the names of those officers whose conversations you took down?

A. Between Lord Brudenell and Captain Rose, Paymaster Leech, Captain Wathen, and Lieutenant Naylor; that was all to my recollection.

Q. Were those officers conversing with Lord Brudenell in presence of each other, or were they singly with his Lordship?

A. They were separate conversations.

Q. As regards both men and horses, did you perceive any difference in the discipline and general appearance of any troop of the 15th Hussars compared with the others; if so, state what that difference was, and in what troop or troops it existed?

A. I did not perceive any difference between the men as far as regards discipline or appearance; as far as regards the horses, as to their appearance, some of those of Captain Wathen's troop did not look so well; in Captain Rose's troop, when the regiment was in Dublin, some of the horses looked as bad.

Q. State to the Court the precise number of horses that looked inferior in Captain Wathen's troop to those of the other troops, and their age.

A. I consider the number to be about six, two out of the six were old; of the remaining four I cannot speak.

Q. Did you conceive the bad appearance of the horses arose from extra work or not?

Lieutenant C. Higginson Teush Hecker's evidence.

A. Not those horses that I have specified.

Q. When you said that latterly there had been more defaulters in Captain Wathen's troop, what period did you allude to?

A. Since the arrival of the regiment in Ireland.

Q. By the prosecutor, through the Court.—After sending for private Surret on the 4th of November, did I not address my observations to him, and not to Captain Wathen?

A. To private Surrett.

Q. Is it not the custom of the regiment, and of the service, for the officer commanding a troop always to attend with any man who wishes to speak to, or is to be spoken to, by the commanding officer?

A. It is the custom of the regiment, and I believe of the service.

Q. When private Surret left the regimental office, what was Captain Wathen's manner in addressing me, and what expressions did he make use of?

A. Captain Wathen's manner was that of a person who felt hurt, and the expression he made use of on private Surrett's leaving the office was, " When you, Lord Brudenell, make such statements respecting my troop, you should bear them out."

Q. Upon Captain Wathen's returning to the regimental office, did I not verbally address him previous to showing or reading the paper alluded to in your evidence?

A. Yes.

Q. Do you recollect what I said to Captain Wathen on that occasion?

A. Lord Brudenell said he did not consider Captain Wathen's manner improper in addressing him in the way he had done?

Q. Do you recollect what was Captain Wathen's reply?

A. Captain Wathen said he was not aware that his manner had been improper.

Lieutenant C. Higginson Teush Hecker's evidence.

Q. Do you recollect what Lord Brudenell said immediately in reply?

A. I do not.

Q. With reference to your evidence of yesterday, has there been one single field day within the last five or six weeks?

A. No.

Q. How many mounted parades have there been in that time for drill?

A. About six.

Q. Since about the 10th of last month, have there been either mounted drills of any sort, or even riding school, except for a few young officers?

A. No; I wish to explain an answer which I gave yesterday, that there had been three field days a-week, at which I attended, and on the intermediate days, skirmishing drill; that answer referred to the weekly drill during the regimental period for field exercise.

Q. How many field days a-week were there during the first six weeks after we came into these barracks, about the 13th of last August?

A. As far as my recollection goes, for the first fortnight after the arrival of the regiment in these quarters, there were none; for the other month, I should say that the average was three a-week.

Q. How many forms of returns of troop debts are usually made out for an inspection in this district?

A. One.

Q. You have said that Captain Wathen placed himself in front of the centre of his troop in trotting past; where were you at that moment?

Lieutenant C. Higginson TeushHecker's evidence.

A. A short distance from the rear of Captain Wathen's troop.

Q. Previous to the inspection, did you hear me repeatedly find fault with the grooming of the horses of any particular troop at every watering parade?

A. At most watering parades Lord Brudenell did remark on the grooming of Captain Wathen's horses, and found fault with them.

Serjeant-Major James Thom's evidence.

Fifth witness for the Prosecution, Serjeant-Major James Thom, of Captain Wathen's troop, was duly sworn and examined on the second charge.

Q. State distinctly to the Court whether, previous to the day of inspection on the 8th of November last, you reported to Captain Wathen that the men of his troop had expressed discontent at the issue of new stable-jackets.

A. I did not.

Q. With reference to an unusual supply of new stable-jackets, how many were charged in the ledger of Captain Wathen's troop previous to the inspection on the 8th of November?

A. Eleven during the year 1833, ten of which were charged during the month of November immediately previous to the inspection.

Cross-examined.

Q. Has there been an unusual issue and charge for stable-jackets and cloth overalls within the last twelve-months to the men of my troop?

A. There has, from what I can trace from the troop ledgers and my own private knowledge.

Serjeant-Major James Thom's evidence.

Q. Was the issue of these articles in the months of September and October a very unusual supply?

A. Yes, I think so.

Q. Was it possible to pay for such issue, and keep the troop debt within the regulation?

A. No.

Q. Did you mention the circumstance to me?

A. Yes.

Q. Did I in consequence pay the bill of the regimental tailor, there being no stoppages sufficient to cover it?

A. Yes.

Q. Have you found it difficult, for some time past, to keep down the debt of the troop?

A. I have.

Q. What has been the reason?

A. The unusual supply of articles from the tailors.

Q. Was the lieutenant-colonel in the habit of inquiring, previous to ordering new jackets or cloth overalls, if the men were in debt?

A. Not of me.

Q. Are any of the men who have been ordered these articles much in debt?

A. Yes.

Q. Who are they?

A. Privates Sims, Allen, Ambler, Wilkinson, Burgess, Hyatt, Saunders, and Surret. I can't recollect more.

Q. Have any of the men had two pair of cloth overalls charged to them within the year?

A. Yes.

Q. Any who had cloth overalls and no stable-jacket?

A. All who have had stable-jackets during the year, have had cloth overalls charged to them.

Q. At Manchester there was a general issue of cloth

Serjeant-Major James Thom's evidence.

overalls charged to the men. Had such an occurrence ever previously taken place since you have been in the regiment?

A. No.

Q. When the major-general was in the regimental office, on the 8th November, were you desired to bring in my mess book, and did you do so?

A. Yes.

Q. By the Court.—Were the men dissatisfied, although they might not complain to Captain Wathen; or did they complain to you?

A. I have overheard words which tended to show that they were dissatisfied; but they did not complain to me.

Serjeant W. Clarkson's evidence.

Sixth witness for the Prosecution, Serjeant Walter Clarkson, of Captain Wathen's troop, was duly sworn and examined on the second charge.

Q. State distinctly to the Court whether, previous to the day of inspection on the 8th of November, you reported to Captain Wathen that the men of his troop had expressed discontent at the issue of new stable-jackets?

A. No.

[Prisoner declined cross-examining this witness.]

Q. By the Court.—Have you any reason to suppose that the men of Captain Wathen's troop were dissatisfied at the issue made to them of new stable-jackets, although they might not have complained to Captain Wathen; or did they complain to you?

A. I have reason to suppose that they were dissatisfied; they did not complain to me, but I heard them express their dissatisfaction.

Seventh witness for the Prosecution, Corporal and Lance-Serjeant John Denby, of Captain Wathen's troop, being duly sworn and examined on the second charge. Corporal John Denby's evidence.

Q. State distinctly to the Court whether, previous to the day of inspection on the 8th of November last, you reported to Captain Wathen that the men of his troop had expressed discontent at the issue of new stable-jackets?

A. No.

Cross-examined by the Prisoner.

Q. Are you not anxious to be promoted?

A. Yes.

Q. Under supposition that you should be so promoted, did you not once buy the crown for your arm?

A. No.

Q. Do you suppose that I have been the occasion of your not being promoted?

A. No.

Q. Did you ever say you thought I was the cause of it?

A. No.

Q. Did you ever mention the circumstance to any one?

A. Yes.

Q. To whom?

A. To the best of my knowledge, to Serjeant-Major Thom.

Q. What did you say?

A. I told Serjeant-Major Thom, after Captain Wathen had released me from confinement to my room one day, that he had intended to stop my promotion; but that on account of my good character since I have been in the troop, Captain Wathen would think no more of it,

Corporal John Denby's evidence.

and that he had sent my name in for promotion in the return of the 31st of August last.

Q. At what time did you consider that I had stopped your promotion?

A. About the middle of August.

Q. On or about the 10th of October, did you not say to Amelia Teeteer, when speaking of me, "He stopped my promotion, may be I'll stop his?"

A. No.

Q. Do you recollect going on talking and saying to Amelia Teeteer, "Aye, stop a bit, one good turn deserves another?"

A. No.

Q. By the Court.—Have you any reason to suppose that the men of Captain Wathen's troop were dissatisfied at the issue of new stable-jackets made to them, although they might not have complained to Captain Wathen; or did they complain to you?

A. I have no reason for supposing that the men were dissatisfied; they did not complain to me.

Captain And. Wood's evidence.

Eighth witness for the Prosecution, Captain Andrew Wood, of the 15th Hussars, being duly sworn, was examined to the first charge.

Q. Had you the command of Captain Wathen's troop during parts of September and October last?

A. Yes.

Q. With reference to the first charge, at parades, in stable dress, did I not usually inspect the stable-jackets of the men, and order those which appeared unfit for wear to be brought to the regimental-office to be again inspected?

A. Yes.

Cross-examined.

Captain And. Wood's evidence.

Q. Who called you into the orderly-room when your books were inspected by the major-general?

A. I was not called in.

Q. Did not the issue of jackets and overalls to my troop during the time you had charge of it appear unusual?

A. It did not.

Q. Did you know what number of jackets and overalls were issued and charged to my men?

A. No.

Q. Did the lieutenant-colonel inquire of you if the men for whom articles were ordered were in debt?

A. No.

Q. Did the serjeant-major of your own troop report to you that he could not pay the tailor without you advanced the money?

A. He did.

Q. Did you advance the money?

A. I did.

Q. Were the charges for jackets and overalls issued previous to the 8th of November, inserted in your ledger?

A. No.

Cross-examination finished.

Q. By the Court. Were any stable-jackets or overalls (those the men paid for) issued to the men of Captain Wathen's troop whilst you had charge of it, without your knowledge or concurrence?

A. Not any.

Q. Had you any previous intimation given to you by the

Captain And. Wood's evidence.

lieutenant-colonel, that such stable-jackets were to be issued; and if so, how long before?

A. I had; his Lordship used to point out the men who wanted stable-jackets to me on parade.

Captain Augustus Fred. Blythe's evidence.

Ninth witness for the Prosecution, Captain Augustus Frederick Blythe, of the 15th Hussars, was duly sworn and examined on the first charge.

Q. Were you adjutant of the regiment some time since?

A. Yes.

Q. Be so good as to state what you know as to the custom in the regiment, with regard to the issue of stable-jackets to be paid for by the men?

A. It has always been the custom in the regiment, when the men's jackets have become too shabby to appear on parade, for new ones to be issued to them at their own expense.

Q. Can you state what number have upon an average been usually issued to a troop in two years?

A. I cannot.

[It being four o'clock, the Court adjourned to eleven o'clock on the following day.]

Saturday, January 1.—*Captain Blythe's examination resumed.*

Q. Previous to the 8th of November last what was your impression as to the supply of stable-jackets in your troop?

A. I did not consider it unusual.

Q How many stable-jackets had been issued to your men previous to the 8th of November last?

A. Nine.

Q. Where was your troop ledger on the day of inspection, on the 8th of November last?

Captain Augustus Fred. Blythe's evidence.

A. To the best of my recollection, it was at Fermoy.

Cross-examination.

Q. You have said you did not think the issue of stable-jackets unusual; what number were issued between the 1st of January 1827 and 31st of December 1831?

A. I have no means of ascertaining exactly what number had been issued during that period.

Q. How then do you judge the late issue not to be unusual?

A. I have already stated that I knew it to be the custom to have the jackets issued to the men as they required them. According to the old system of arrears, and two monthly settlements, a man at the end of that period, if prudent and careful, would have a considerable amount to receive, and in that case men would frequently prefer paying for the article themselves, to having it entered against them in the ledgers.

Q. Do you mean to say that the number of jackets issued were not unusual?

A. As in my former answer I have stated that I had no means of ascertaining the number which had been issued on previous occasions, I cannot of course say whether the number issued during the year 1833 was unusual or not.

Q. What number have you returned in the statement made out for my use, as issued from 1827 to 1831?

A. Only two.

Q. When were the overalls, stated in your troop return to be issued in 1832, charged in your ledger?

A. I really do not recollect.

Captain Augustus Fred. Blythe's evidence.

Q. Were they charged in that year?

A. I really do not know; I was not captain of the troop in that year.

Q. By your return it appears that fourteen stable-jackets, issued since October, are not charged to the men; what is the reason?

A. By referring to that return, I think you will find that five only have not been charged, those five have been issued since October. The bills have not been sent in; the men are now put under stoppages for them.

Q. When you were adjutant was it the custom of the regiment to take down in writing the conversation between the commanding officer and the officers?

A. No.

Q. How long since you have heard of such custom being adopted?

A. I never heard of it before.

Cross-examination finished.

Q. By the Court. Do you mean to say you are ignorant of such a custom now existing in the 15th Hussars?

A. I now recollect, that for the first time, I heard yesterday in the mess-room the subject discussed.

Q. Please to state if any men of your troop expressed dissatisfaction or discontent at their receiving stable-jackets?

A. When the men's names were first put down who were to receive new stable-jackets, three of them came to me to show me their jackets, saying, that they thought I should, on re-inspection, find them equally good with some of those whose jackets had been only ordered to be repaired; the circumstance was reported, two of the stable-jackets afterwards were decided to be repairable, the third man was ordered to get a new one.

Captain Augustus Fred. Blythe's evidence.

Q. To whom was it reported, and who decided on it?

A. I reported it to the quarter-master, and I cannot say who decided upon it, as a day or two afterwards I went to Fermoy.

Q. In the returns of debts of your troop, given to the major-general, were the stable-jackets issued previous to the 8th of November charged to the men?

A. They were not.

Q. You have stated that the five jackets issued since October last, have not yet been charged, the bills not yet having been sent in; is it not customary for the captain of a troop to certify that his debt and credit return includes all charges his men are liable to?

A. It is the custom.

Q. What is the charge for a stable-jacket of the 15th Hussars?

A. Eighteen shillings.

Q. Is it the custom in the 15th Hussars for the quarter-master to be the judge whether a new stable-jacket is required for a man, or is the captain of his troop left to decide?

A. Neither the one nor the other; the commanding officer would decide.

Q. Who supplies the stable-jackets?

A. The quarter-master.

Q. To whom do captains of troops pay for stable-jackets issued to their men?

A. The money is paid to the quarter-master.

Q. You said there was a discussion in the mess-room yesterday, respecting the conversations of officers in the orderly-room with their commanding officer being taken

Captain Augustus Fred. Blythe's evidence.

down in writing. Pray state decidedly whether you are aware if that custom now exists in the 15th Hussars?

A. I can't say decidedly, but I believe it does.

Q. By the Prosecutor, through the Court. What makes you believe that the custom of taking down conversations exists in the regiment?

A. From the conversations that I heard in the mess-room, and from the evidence given by Mr. Hecker on the subject.

Q. Have you been stationed lately with your troop, and has your troop been altogether broken up since the service troops were formed?

A. I have not been lately with my troop, and my troop has been broken up since the service squadrons were first formed.

Quarter-Master George Chettle's evidence.

Tenth witness for the Prosecution, Quarter Master George Chettle, of the 15th Hussars, was duly sworn and examined as to the first charge.

Q. How long have you been in the 15th Hussars?

A. Near thirty-four years.

Q. What has been the custom of the regiment, as to the issue of new stable-jackets to the men, as their old ones became unfit for wear?

A. It has been the custom of the men to obtain orders from the serjeant-major, or officer commanding the troop, to the tailor, for their being issued.

Q. Previous to the day of inspection, in what proportion did you tell me that new stable-jackets had been usually issued to the men in two years, to be paid for by themselves?

Quarter-Master George Chettle's evidence.

A. I supposed about one-third of the number of men with the regiment.

Q. Did you give the same account to the major-general?

A. I did.

Q. How many new stable-jackets had been recently issued to the men of the regiment, previous to the 8th of November last?

A. Sixty.

Q. Do you consider an issue of new stable jackets during the two years to be necessary?

A. For a number of the men, it is.

Q. What was the custom of the regiment relative to the issue of new stable-jackets when Lieutenant-Colonel Thackwell commanded the regiment?

A. As a jacket became of no further use, it was replaced by the master-tailor, at the expense of the dragoon.

Q. Were the accounts for the payment of the new stable-jackets alluded to, sent into the captains of troops by you?

A. For thirty-seven of them—the accounts were sent to each troop.

Q. Did you send the account to Captain Wathen's troop?

A. I did.

Q. Do you consider that the supply of new stable-jackets, within the last two years, has been an unusual one in point of number?

A. As far as I have the means of judging, I should say not.

Q. How many new stable-jackets have been issued up to the present date?

A. Eighty.

Q. Is it not unusual for you to send the accounts for

Quarter-Master George Chettle's evidence.

stable-jackets charged as articles of necessaries to the captains of troops?

A. Quite so.

Q. How did it occur on that occasion to which you have referred?

A. The person employed as a master-tailor being about to leave the regiment, he gave me an account of the number of stable-jackets he had provided, which accounts I sent to the troops.

Cross-examination.

Q. Are the two returns marked C. and D. now shown to you, true statements of the issues to the several troops for the periods stated?

A. That marked C. I believe to be correct; the one marked D. is only an extract from a return sent by a late master-tailor, of which it is a correct copy as to numbers.

[These returns, marked C. and D., are now transmitted with these proceedings.]

Q. You have said the issue of stable-jackets at former periods amounted to about one-third of the regiment; what has been the proportion in the two last years?

A. About one-fourth.

Q. Did you not tell the general it was only one-sixth?

A. I did—about that number, at the time the question was put to me, having been issued.

Q. Your return to me states the number of jackets from 1827 to 1831, to be twenty-one, and from 1832 to 1833 to be eighty; how do you reconcile this with the comparison made by you?

A. It is impossible for me to speak as to the correctness of the return marked D., that being only an extract from a statement made by another person. I have no doubt but in that period a number of men bought jackets which the late master-tailor might not have been aware of.

Quarter-Master George Chettle's evidence.

Q. Upon what ground then do you draw your comparison?

A. From a written statement made by Lieutenant-Colonel Thackwell in 1825, and also in 1828.

Q. Have you not been quarter-master during the periods, and ought you not to know from your own knowledge and books?

A. I have been quarter-master during the whole of the periods, but have never been called upon to take an account of jackets issued from the tailor for which the men were to pay.

Q. How many stable-jackets were issued to my troop in the year 1833, and how many from 1827 to 1831?

A. In the year 1833, seventeen; and five from 1827 to 1831.

Q. Were the stable-jackets and overalls issued to my troop during the year 1833 furnished with my knowledge?

A. I cannot say.

Q. What is the price of a pair of cloth overalls in the 15th Hussars?

A. Eighteen shillings and eleven-pence.

Cross-examination finished.

Q. *By the Court.* Do you supply cloth for the stable-jackets?

A. I do not generally, but on occasion of the stable-jackets in question, I did supply the cloth.

Q. How many jackets did you furnish cloth for, from 1832 to 1833?

A. Thirty-seven.

Quarter-Master George Chettle's evidence.

Q. What proportion of that number was for Captain Wathen's troop?

A. Ten.

Q. When did you send to Captain Wathen the account alluded to in your evidence, for stable-jackets issued to his troop, and what was the number specified in that account?

A. I believe about the middle of October, and the number specified was ten.

Q. Did you send to the other captains of troops their accounts at the same time you sent Captain Wathen's?

A. I did.

Q. By the Prosecutor through the Court. How did it happen that you supplied the cloth on the late issue of stable-jackets?

A. Having a saving of cloth from the last clothing in the colonel's store, it was made use of for that purpose.

Private Geo. Chester's evidence.

Eleventh witness for the Prosecution, Private George Chester, tailor of the 15th Hussars, was duly sworn, and examined to the first charge.

Q. How long have you been a working tailor in the 15th Hussars?

A. About nineteen years.

Q. With reference to the issue of new stable-jackets, how many have been on an average, taking the last six or eight years, issued to each troop in the regiment during the two years which those paid for by the colonel are supposed to be kept in wear?

A. I should think from fifteen to twenty.

Q. Is that in each troop?

A. Yes.

Twelfth witness for the Prosecution, Lieutenant-Colonel Alexander Kennedy Clarke, of the 7th Dragoon Guards, was duly sworn, and examined as to the first charge.

Lieutenant-Colonel Alex. Kennedy Clarke's evidence.

Q. Be so good as to state what the custom of your regiment is, with regard to new stable-jackets being issued to the men at their own expense?

A. When the regular assignment of clothing provided for by the General is become shabby and nearly worn out, it is customary for the officers commanding troops to give in a return to the regimental quarter-master, of those men they consider should be provided with new jackets; which return is given to the master-tailor, who orders cloth and makes them according to that return, and they are regularly charged in the men's accounts accordingly.

Q. What number of new stable-jackets have been issued to the men of your regiment within the last two years?

A. To the best of my belief since the 1st of March last to the 30th of November, 231—and since that period, three or four more—this includes non-commissioned officers.

Q. From your own experience can you say what is the custom of the service generally on those points?

A. As far as two regiments are concerned, I consider it the custom for the men to be supplied with stable-jackets as they require them.

Q. What is the custom of your regiment with regard to a general issue of new overalls, to be paid for by the men?

A. They are issued as required.

Cross-examination.

Q. Do you not conceive, that as scarlet cloth is more easily stained than blue, the stable-jackets may oftener

Lieutenant-Colonel Alex. Kennedy Clarke's evidence.

require to be replaced by new in your regiment, than in the King's Hussars?

A. I should think it probable.

Q. How many cloth overalls upon an average are issued and charged to the men per year, in each troop in your regiment?

A. I consider that the duty men require one pair every two years.

Q. Do you consider it regular for articles of necessaries or clothing to be issued without the knowledge of the captain or officer in charge of troops?

A. No.

Q. Is it customary in the 7th Dragoon Guards for the adjutant to take down, in writing, the conversations in the orderly-room, between the commanding officer and the officers, or have you ever known or heard of such a system in any other regiment in the service?

A. It is not customary in the 7th Dragoon Guards. I have heard of such things many years ago, but I have never known it.

Q. *By the Court.*—Is it the custom in your regiment to place men under stoppages before issuing new stable-jackets or cloth overalls?

A. Yes, in compliance with the last clothing warrant?

Quarter-Master John Johnston's evidence.

Thirteenth witness for the Prosecution, Regimental Quarter-Master John Johnston, of the 7th Dragoon Guards, was duly sworn, and examined on the first charge.

Q. Were you not formerly in the 15th Hussars?

A. Yes.

Q. What was the custom of that regiment at that time, as to the issue of new stable-jackets to the men at their own expense?

A. I am not aware that there was any issue of stable-jackets in the 15th Hussars? Quarter-Master John Johnston's evidence.

Cross-examination.

Q. Please to state the number of years you were in the King's Hussars, and the number of stable-jackets you paid for during that time?

A. I was in the 15th Hussars from August, 1813, to April, 1824, and during that time I paid for one stable-jacket.

Q. Do you not think that from the difference of the colour, the men of the 7th Dragoon Guards would require more stable-jackets than those of the King's Hussars?

A. Yes.

Fourteenth witness for the Prosecution, Lieutenant-Colonel Chatterton, of the 4th Dragoon Guards, a member of the Court, was duly sworn, and examined on the first charge. Lieutenant-Colonel Chatterton's evidence.

Q. What is the custom in your regiment as to the issue of new stable-jackets?

A. It is the custom of the 4th Dragoon Guards for the men to be supplied with new stable-jackets, at their own expense, whenever they require them.

Q. What is the custom of the service on that point?

A. In two of the cavalry regiments, in which I have served, the 12th Lancers and 7th Dragoon Guards, such is the custom.

Cross-examination.

Q. Is it customary in the 4th Dragoon Guards for the adjutant to take down in writing the conversations in the orderly-room, between the officer commanding and the

Lieutenant-Colonel Chatterton's evidence.

officers, or have you ever known or heard of such a system in any other regiment of the service?

A. It is not customary in the 4th Dragoon Guards, nor have I ever known or heard of it being practised in any regiment in his Majesty's service with the exception of what has appeared before this court.

Lieutenant-Colonel Lord Brudenell's evidence.

Fifteenth witness for the Prosecution, Lieutenant-Colonel Lord Brudenell, of the 15th Hussars, was duly sworn and examined.

Q. By the Judge-Advocate.—With reference to the first charge, have the goodness to state to the Court what took place in your Lordship's presence in the orderly-room on the 8th of November.

A. On the afternoon of the 8th of November last, Major-General Sir Thomas Arbuthnot inspected the troop books of the regiment in the orderly-room. After he had looked at the books of Captain Wathen's troop, and at the time that Captain Wathen ought to have retired, Captain Wathen commenced voluntarily to say to the major-general, "Sir, I conclude that Lord Brudenell has made a complaint about my troop debt." The major-general immediately said, "Captain Wathen, Lord Brudenell has made no complaint whatever about your troop debt." Captain Wathen then said, that the excess above the regulation, or the amount, or words to that effect, arose from an unusual supply of new stable-jackets, which had been sent from the tailor's shop without his knowledge, and he scarcely knew by whose orders. The major-general immediately inquired of him, whether he meant to say, that the new stable-jackets were unnecessary. Captain Wathen replied, that they were, and that, in his opinion, the old

Lieutenant-Colonel Lord Brudenell's evidence.

ones would have lasted the time. Upon being further questioned by the major-general, he said, that the issue of jackets had caused discontent amongst his men; and upon being further asked by the major-general, how he was aware that that was the case, he said, that the serjeants had reported the circumstance to him, and that he had reported or mentioned the circumstance to me, his commanding officer; upon which I said, "Captain Wathen never said one word to me on the subject." The major-general then went on to make more particular inquiry into the subject, adding, as far as I can recollect, that it was his duty so to do. Captain Wathen, in reply, deliberately stated again, that the serjeants had reported to him that his men had expressed discontent, and that he had mentioned or reported the circumstance to me; upon which, in a moment of surprise and indignation at such an assertion, which I knew to be contrary to the fact, I said, "Sir, this is a fal— unfounded statement." The major-general immediately desired Captain Wathen to retire; and he then said to me, "Lord Brudenell, what an expression you were very near making use of to Captain Wathen! I request you will not interrupt me again when I am speaking to an officer." Captain Wathen then re-entered. The major-general may have said some other words; that is all I can recollect; very little more was then said, and what was said I do not recollect upon the above subject. I accompanied the major-general to a parade under arms in the barrack-yard: shortly after the parade, Captain Wathen was sent for again to the regimental-office, which was about one hour from the time of his having made the above statement. The major-general then told him, that it was his duty to make particular inquiries into the subject of the discontent of his men; upon which Captain Wathen told him, that he had

Lieutenant-Colonel Lord Brudenell's evidence.

never said his men were discontented. The major-general reminded him, that he had said the serjeants had reported to him that the men were discontented; upon which Captain Wathen, in a very disrespectful manner, gave a flat denial to the major-general. About this time the captains of troops were sent for to the orderly-room; and upon the major-general asking them individually, first, whether they considered the supply of stable-jackets in their troops unusual, and secondly, whether their men had expressed any discontent on the subject, they all replied in the negative to both questions. The major-general then said, "Captain Wathen, I must say, I think it rather extraordinary, when I am so much pleased with every thing I have seen, and expressed my approbation on all points," or words to that effect, "that you should have come forward to make that statement, in, I must say"—to the best of my belief, the word was—"ungracious manner towards your commanding officer." Captain Wathen then said, "Why, sir, almost every man in my troop is under stoppages for these articles." I said, "Sir, I do not think this can be the case," for it was but a very short time since, that I sent for the serjeant-major of his troop, to know whether all the men who were in debt, were placed under stoppages; as there appeared to me to be few or fewer than there ought to be. I ordered the mess-book to be sent for, but it was not shown to the major-general. I forgot to mention, that on the occasion of Captain Wathen making one reply to the major-general, he said, "Excuse me, general, you must have been mistaken, or misunderstood me, as to my having said that the men were discontented." Captain Rose, at this interview at the office, said, he thought it fair to state to the major-general, that the stable-jackets were not charged in his troop ledger, which I now state to the Court, was the first time I had ever heard any thing on the subject of stable-jackets being charged in some troop ledgers and not in others. After the captains of troops leaving the room, Captain Ives returned and said, he also thought it right to tell the major-general that the stable-jackets were not charged in his troop ledger. Captain Wathen, some time during this interview, told the major-general, that I had recently told him, Captain Wathen, that his troop, up to a short time previous to the inspection, was the worst in the regiment: I said in the major-general's presence, "Well, and was it not the case?"

Lieutenant-Colonel Lord Brudenell's evidence.

Q. By the Judge Advocate. State all you know respecting the second charge.

A. On the Monday following the 11th of November, Major-General Sir Thomas Arbuthnot having ordered a parade for the inspection of necessaries in the barrack-yard, after he had finished inspecting some infantry, desired me to send for Captain Wathen. Upon Captain Wathen's arriving, the major-general told him that he wished to see a serjeant, or the serjeants, or words to that effect, I forget which, who had reported to Captain Wathen that the men had expressed discontent; upon which Captain Wathen answered, "Sir, if you recollect," or words to that effect, "I told you on Friday last that the men were not discontented." Upon which the major-general said, "Surely, Captain Wathen, you told me that your serjeants had reported to you that your men had expressed discontent at the issue of new stable-jackets; and I appeal to Lord Brudenell, Captain Corkran, and Colonel Turner, whether that was not the case." I immediately said, "Sir, he distinctly and most positively stated it," or words to that effect. Captain Wathen, at either one or other of these interviews, said, that I had taunted him with the amount of his troop

Lieutenant-Colonel Lord Brudenell's evidence.

debt, and that that had very much irritated him. We almost immediately went to the other side of the officers' building, for the parade for the inspection of necessaries.

Q. By the Judge Advocate.—With reference to the third charge, state all you know to the Court.

A. I can most positively state, that Captain Wathen did not, previous to the inspection, either report, mention, or say one word to me upon the subject of discontent amongst his men.

Q. By the Judge Advocate.—With reference to the first charge, state how many stable-jackets were charged in the ledger of Captain Wathen's troop.

A. From my own personal examination within the last few days, nine jackets were charged to privates and one to a serjeant, previous to the settling day before the inspection. I did not examine the troop ledgers myself previous to the inspection; I sent them to the senior major for that purpose, who reported to me officially in writing, which report I have now in my possession, and now produce to the Court, that they—[this document marked letter G was read to the Court, and now accompanies these proceedings]—were all correct. On the following morning, Saturday, to the best of my recollection, I enclosed the remarks in the return of troop debts against Captain Rose's troop, as mentioned in that return.

Cross-examination.

Q. Did your Lordship, in the orderly-room, on the 7th of November, remark upon the debt of my troop being larger than that of other captains?

A. I told Captain Wathen that his debt was the largest, and I asked him the reason of it.

Q. Did I explain the cause of its appearing so?

A. Captain Wathen said that it arose from the great number of articles which had been issued for the outfit for service, stable-jackets, overalls, &c.

Lieutenant-Colonel Lord Brudenell's evidence.

Q. Had you not then received debt and credit lists from the troops for the month of September?

A. Of course I had.

Q. Had you not thereby perceived that the debt of some other troop or troops was very much greater than mine?

Q. The subject never occurred to me on the 7th of November; I have since looked at the debts and credits of some of the troops for the month of September, and to the best of my recollection, there is a debt against one troop of £40.

Q. Did you not know that it was impossible that they could so suddenly be reduced below mine, and consequently that the jackets could not have been charged?

A. Nothing of the sort occurred to me at the time, as far as relates to a comparison between the troop debts.

Q. Did you ever countenance the charges for articles furnished to the troops, being withheld by the quartermaster or master tailor?

A. To the best of my recollection I never heard or said a word on the subject.

Q. At the inspection of the regiment, was there more than one man of my troop who preferred a complaint to the major-general?

A. Only one I believe, private Surrett, and that totally unconnected with the present charges.

Q. Was not the time of the books being inspected the proper time for me to explain the cause of my debt to the major-general?

A. I consider that as the major-general either told you

Lieutenant-Colonel Lord Brudenell's evidence.

that he was satisfied, or bowed to you to retire, that it was both unnecessary and improper that you should agitate the subject.

Q. Did I not tell the major-general you had warned me I should have to explain the cause of my debt?

A. Captain Wathen did so; *but I never had warned him to that effect.*

Q. Why was the mess-book not shown to the major-general?

A. Because he did not ask for it, and went away to dinner.

Q. Please to say when you first heard any thing concerning the stable-jackets not being charged in other troop ledgers?

A. On the afternoon of the 8th of November, when Captain Rose reported to the major-general that they were not charged in his ledger.

Q. Did I not, in presence of the adjutant, on the 7th of November, say that the debt of another troop, compared with mine, was perhaps small, in consequence of the stable-jackets not being charged in that troop ledger?

A. I asked you why your troop debt was so much larger than Captain Ives' troop debt; you first said, " I have nothing to do with the debts of other troops;" and you then said, " May be, all the articles are not charged in those debts, but I can know nothing about that;" you did not specify stable-jackets particularly.

Q. Your having inscribed opposite my troop debt that you did not consider my reasons for the excess of debt were sufficient, was it not my duty to satisfy the major-general on that subject?

A. When you made that statement to the major-general, no remarks had been inserted in the return of troop debts.

Q. Were there not twenty-seven men of my troop under stoppages at the time you sent for the mess-book to contradict my statement to the major-general? Lieutenant-Colonel Lord Brudenell's evidence.

A. There were twenty-five men under full stoppages, and about two or three more for sixpence or a shilling, out of forty-five men of your own troop; there were about nine-and-twenty men under stoppages, out of about sixty men, of which the service troop was composed, and of which you had the command.

Q. Had my accounts any thing to do with other troops, or the sixty men of the service troop?

A. No.

Q. On the 4th of November, when I said I had not been aware that my words were taken down, did your Lordship reply, "I dare say not, Sir, but I find it very convenient?"

A. I have no recollection of having said, "I find it very convenient;" when you said your conduct had not been insubordinate and improper, I told you that the expressions you had made use of had been taken down.

Q. When your Lordship had procured my words to be taken down during the discussion, after private Surrett had left the office, what use did you intend to make of them?

A. No other use whatever than that to which I turned them; namely, when you returned to the office, and said that your conduct and expressions had not been insubordinate and improper, I told you I had the best proof that they were so, for your words were taken down.

Q. Did you not speak to the major-general previous to the inspection, relative to a man of my troop who declined signing his accounts? and did you not prepare him for some complaints that might be made?

Lieutenant-Colonel Lord Brudenell's evidence.

A. There was one man in Captain Wathen's troop, private Surrett, and one man in Captain Blythe's troop, who had, previous to the inspection, refused to sign their accounts for the same cause. I mentioned the subject to the major-general, who said, he should refer the cases to Dublin, and to the War-office, both of which courses have been adopted.

Q. On the 4th of November, after private Surrett left the office, did I not request you to bring before the major-general the state of my troop, which you had, in private Surrett's presence, termed the worst in the regiment, indeed in the service?

A. Yes, in the manner following. After private Surrett left the regimental office, you addressed me in a very menacing and insubordinate manner in my opinion, saying, "Sir, when you think proper to bring such charges against a troop, I beg you will substantiate them."

Q. Did you inform the major-general that my words had been taken down?

A. I have no recollection of having said any thing to the major-general on the subject.

Q. Did you offer any atonement to me for the insult conveyed in the syllable "fal," which you have admitted having used?

A. Certainly not, and for the following reasons. When an officer and a gentleman deliberately repeats a second time that which was totally contrary to truth and fact, the syllable I made use of was undoubtedly improper; but if I had sufficient sense of propriety within myself to correct myself before I gave utterance to a word of one syllable, I think, under the extraordinary aggravation of the case, no further apology was required of me, particularly as the major-general said nothing on the subject.

Q. Was it not by signal made to you by the major-general holding up his hand, as he has stated in this Court, that you stopped at the syllable "fal?"

Lieutenant-Colonel Lord Brudenell's evidence.

A. Certainly not; I corrected myself. I have no recollection of the major-general putting up his hand.

Q. When did you first instruct the adjutant to take down the conversations in the orderly-room?

A. I never gave any order on that subject to be generally adopted. For a year and a half I have been in the habit of constantly and even daily communicating with officers under my command, both upon points of duty and otherwise; and there never has been one word put down by my order or otherwise, in any conversations on duty or otherwise, between myself and either of the two majors, or myself and four out of six captains, or myself and twelve out of fourteen subalterns, or between myself and four out of five staff officers. The order, or rather the wish, which I expressed to Lieutenant and Adjutant Hecker about August 1832, arose out of a particular circumstance, and was only to be observed under particular circumstances. The occurrence which gave rise to the above directions, which I gave to the adjutant, was, to the best of my recollection, the extremely disrespectful and improper conduct of a staff officer of my regiment in the orderly-room. After he had left the office, I requested the adjutant to commit to paper what had occurred, as that matter had all the appearance of being likely to give rise to ulterior measures. I thought then, and I think now, that it was the most fair course to adopt to prevent any unjust accusation, or any mistake, being made as to what had occurred. Some other conversation between the same staff officer and myself may very probably have been taken down during the winter of 1832. When the regiment arrived in Dublin, I had an

Lieutenant-Colonel Lord Brudenell's evidence.

unfortunate difference with one of my captains; the case was referred to Sir Hussey Vivian; that captain and myself had an interview in the orderly-room, at which no other person was present; he declared that one thing was said there; I thought and said that the direct reverse was said. During that dispute, which lasted some time before it was adjusted, I thought it right and proper, and therefore ordered, that every thing which I said to him, or he said to me, on the subject of that dispute, should be committed to writing; that course was openly adopted when I addressed him in presence of the captains and field officers of the regiment; that dispute was adjusted by Sir Hussey Vivian. The next occasion upon which words were taken down after the officer had left the orderly-room, was in those barracks in the first week of September last, when the same staff officer, to whom I have before alluded, conducted himself again in an extremely disrespectful, and I must say, insubordinate manner; it is just possible that that officer's words may have been taken down again. A subaltern officer's conversation with me was taken down in his own aid and assistance. The adjutant, I believe, put down the words of one other subaltern, when he was angry. Excepting those, and with the exception of Captain Wathen, not one word that any other officer ever addressed to me during nearly two years that I have been in the command of the regiment, and always present with them, has ever been put down.

Q. Were the officers made aware that their conversation was to be taken down in writing?

A. Certainly not; if I had told any officer that that was to be the case, I must also have said, beware of not being insubordinate, to account for it.

Cross-examination finished.

Lieutenant-Colonel Lord Brudenell's evidence.

Q. *By the Court.*—When you ordered the adjutant to take down in writing what Captain Wathen said, did you at the same time request him to write down what you said after Captain Wathen had left the room?

A. Upon the few occasions on which the adjutant has ever taken down what an officer stated to me, he also at the same time put down the words I had addressed to the officer. The adjutant did not put down my conversation with him, the adjutant, after Captain Wathen left the office, but always what I addressed to the officer.

Q. How was the adjutant to know when he was to take down the conversation between you and your officers?

A. Upon the occasions of the insubordinate and disrespectful conduct to which I have alluded, on the officer's leaving the office, I have said to the adjutant, "You had better take down all that occurred, to prevent mistakes."

Q. Why did you make a remark opposite to the debt of Captain Wathen, and not to that of the other troops, before the communication was made to the major-general?

A. Because, in every way that you may consider it, it was the largest debt in the regiment unaccounted for; a remark to that effect was also made on the second return.

Q. When you made the remark regarding Captain Wathen's troop, were you aware that the debt of some of the other troops exceeded ten pounds.

A. Of course I was.

Q. You have stated, the major-general told Captain Wathen his conduct was ungracious towards his commanding officer; did you consider that he intended to reprimand him?

A. Most certainly not.

Lieutenant-Colonel Lord Brudenell's evidence.

Q. Can you state to the court, that you have not in any instance been actuated by a hostile feeling towards Captain Wathen, but such as you would have done to any other officer in the regiment under your command?

A. After an officer has systematically thwarted and opposed me for two or three months together, in addition to, as I think, unjustly reporting me, I will not pretend to say that my feelings towards that officer are the same as towards one who has conducted himself regularly; but I have always treated him, Captain Wathen, as I think fairly—but this is for the Court to judge of.

Q. Can you state that your feelings, in any instance, towards Captain Wathen, have not influenced you in the discharge of your public duty as commanding officer of the regiment?

A. I can positively say, that it has not.

Q. Was the adjutant present in the orderly-room when you termed Captain Wathen's troop the worst in the regiment, and in the service; and when Captain Wathen asked you to bring the state of his troop before the major-general?

A. The adjutant was present on the 4th of November, when addressing private Surret, I blamed the men of Captain Wathen's troop for their idleness and want of care of their horses.

Q. Did this blame apply to Captain Wathen's troop only, or generally to the service troop under his command?

A. Most particularly to the men of Captain Wathen's troop; blame was in some degree to be attached to the men of the other troop placed under his command.

Q. You have said that Captain Wathen's troop was the worst in the regiment or service; in what respect did it merit that character, beyond want of attention to grooming?

A. I have never admitted here that I said it was the worst troop in the service. I have said that it was the worst troop in the regiment, for the following reasons. I make this statement with deep pain and regret, because I feel that it reflects great discredit on a troop of the regiment I have the honour to command. The extraordinary number of horses with sore backs and broken knees since we came to Ireland, and particularly in these quarters, to such an extent, that when we were in daily expectation of an order for foreign service, as to render the troop in some measure ineffective. Out of forty-five horses, twenty-three have had sore backs since we came to Ireland; about sixteen of which occurred since we came to these quarters—out of six cases of broken horses in the regiment, three have occurred in that troop.

Lieutenant-Colonel Lord Brudenell's evidence.

Q. State to the court how many horses there were in Captain Wathen's troop with sore backs and broken knees more than in any other troop, and if so, what caused them, with the precise time they occurred?

A. Since we came to Ireland, there has been just double the number of sore acks in that troop, within one, that has occurred in any one of the other troops of the regiment; four cases of broken knees out of six, in the regiment, one was in Captain Blythe's, and the other in Captain Wood's troop. I can assign no other cause whatever than the existence of a temporary evil which was spreading like a contagion through the regiment, and required the most prompt and strong measures on my part to put a stop to. I can attribute the evil to no other cause than a temporary fit of idleness and carelessness on the part of the men. This occurred at different times since we came to Ireland.

Lieutenant-Colonel Lord Brudenell's evidence.

Q. Was this evil caused by bad blankets, or carelessness of the men in folding them?

A. In my opinion, not from bad blankets; but, perhaps, from carelessness in folding the blankets, and carelessness in riding on duty.

Q. Do you mean to state positively to the Court, that the carelessness, which you have stated to have existed on the part of the men, together with the sore backs and broken knees, were owing to Captain Wathen's neglect, so far as refers to his troop?

A. I conceive that the extent of the evil, which arose after we had arrived in these barracks, and the continuance of the evil in that troop much longer than it existed in any other in the regiment, proceeded in a great measure from Captain Wathen's want of co-operation with me when I first thought it my duty to adopt strong measures to suppress the existence of an evil so prejudicial to the efficacy of the service squadrons.

Q. Did you consider the non-commissioned officers and subalterns of that troop to be fully competent to the duties of their respective situations; and if so, did you ascertain whether they had performed them?

A. I considered the non-commissioned officers and subalterns competent to perform their duties. I consider it my duty, as commanding officer of the regiment, to speak to the captain commanding a troop as the responsible person. I have no recollection of Captain Wathen having reported any subaltern or non-commissioned officer either inefficient or inactive.

Q. Is that your uniform practice in the regiment?

A. Certainly with regard to the stable duties, and the effective state of the horses.

Q. You have stated that sixteen out of twenty-three cases of sore backs in Captain Wathen's troop occurred since the regiment came to these quarters; how long has Captain Wathen during that period been in the actual every-day charge of his troop?

Lieutenant-Colonel Lord Brudenell's evidence.

A. The whole period, except from about the 18th or 20th of October to the 25th of November, and there has been no sore back in the regiment since the inspection.

Q. You have stated that Captain Wathen, in a very disrespectful manner, gave a flat denial to the major-general. What words did Captain Wathen use?

A. No very objectionable words—"I did not tell you so,"—having reference to the discontent of the men.

Q. Have the King's Hussars been inspected by any general commanding a district except Sir Thomas Arbuthnot, since you assumed the command of the regiment; and if so, did you produce the mess-book on those occasions or not?

A. The regiment has been inspected four times previous to the last inspection—twice by Sir Henry Bouverie, once by Sir Charles Dalbiac, and once by Sir Edward Blakeney—the weekly mess-book has never been looked at on these occasions, not being in the regulated list of books to be shown to a general officer.

Q. Did you state to Major-General Sir Thomas Arbuthnot, that a soldier of the 15th Hussars had grumbled when ordered by you to get his stable-jacket repaired instead of having a new one served out to him; and if so, please to state to the Court his name, and the troop to which he belonged?

A. I did; on Monday, the 11th; private Hopkin, of Captain Wathen's troop.

Q. Did any other soldiers of the 15th, who had been

Lieutenant-Colonel Lord Brudenell's evidence.

marked for new stable-jackets, appear to be dissatisfied therewith, and were they afterwards allowed to have their old ones repaired, instead of having new jackets served out to them?

A. A few men asked to be allowed to have their jackets repaired, of those to whom new ones had been ordered.

Q. From your knowledge of the feelings and dispositions of soldiers, might not the men of Captain Wathen's troop have been dissatisfied, although they could not, or did not, substantiate their real or imaginary grievances?

A. It is possible that they might have been dissatisfied —they certainly could, if they had chosen it, have made any complaint.

Q. During the time you have commanded the 15th Hussars, were the officers commanding troops directed, at any time, to bring forward any ground of complaint or feelings of dissatisfaction amongst the men, however frivolous, in order that every thing of that nature might be investigated at the next inspection?

A. Always to bring every sort of complaint before me, to be treated as I should think proper.

Q. You have stated that the subalterns and non-commissioned officers of Captain Wathen's troop were competent to perform their duty; do you then impute all the blame of bad conduct to Captain Wathen only?

A. The captain of a troop is the responsible person to me. I impute want of zeal and co-operation on the part of Captain Wathen, in order to put a stop to the irregularities I have alluded to.

Q. It appears in evidence that until the information was given by Captain Corkran, it was a matter of doubt to you, whether the explanation respecting the excess of troop debts should be inserted in the return by the commanding officer, or by the officer commanding the troop; might not Captain Wathen have been alike uncertain on that point, and consequently have considered it was a part of his duty to give the explanation at the time his books were inspected by the major-general?

Lieutenant-Colonel Lord Brudenell's evidence.

A. I think not, because he had not been called upon to fill up the return; he had a right, therefore, to suppose it was my duty; he could not, therefore, think it was his.

Q. Can you state whether the men of Captain Wathen's troop, who were in debt, were under stoppages to the extent authorized by the king's warrant of 1831?

A. Excepting one or two cases, which I mentioned yesterday, of stoppages of a shilling or sixpence, they were all under stoppages of three shillings and sixpence a-week, which is to the full extent authorized by any warrant, to the best of my belief, and that is the system of the regiment.

Q. You have stated, that Captain Wathen had systematically thwarted and opposed you. Pray state in what manner he has done so, confining yourself to the period between Captain Wathen's release from his first arrest and his being again placed under arrest?

A. I cannot fairly be limited to that period, having yesterday stated in evidence, that it was during three months; since his release from the first arrest, upon my speaking to a man of his troop, attended by him, according to the established custom of the regiment, in strong terms, relative to the man's misconduct and that of the other men of the troop—that Captain Wathen, in an insubordinate and menacing manner, telling me that if I brought such charges against the troop I should substantiate them, comes under

Lieutenant-Colonel Lord Brudenell's evidence.

the head of thwarting and opposing a commanding officer, in my opinion.

Q. Should you have preferred the three first charges against Captain Wathen, had it not been for the circumstance contained in the allegations of the fourth, fifth, and sixth charges?

A. I was under the guidance of the major-general of the district, and it depended upon instructions which I might have received from him.

Q. What time elapsed from the time of Captain Wathen's denying that discontent existed in his troop, and his being put in arrest; and when was it intimated to him that charges would be preferred against him?

A. Captain Wathen first gave that denial after returning from parade on the 8th of November last; he repeated that denial on the Monday following, the 11th; and he was placed in arrest on Tuesday, the 12th; the charges approved by the general commanding-in-chief, were transmitted to me on the 8th of December, and immediately given to Captain Wathen. I beg to add, that to the best of my recollection, it had been previously notified by me to Captain Wathen that charges would be preferred against him, certainly that the whole matter had been forwarded to head-quarters.

Q. You have stated that Captain Wathen was in actual command of his troop during the whole period of the regiment being in these quarters, with the exception of from about the 18th or 20th of October to the 25th of November; be so good as to state when Captain Wathen was first placed in arrest, and when released?

A. In my former answer as to the dates of the first arrest, I made a mistake in the month; it was on the 25th of September, and not on the 18th or 20th of October, that he was placed under arrest, and it was on the 20th of October, and not on the 25th of November, that he was released.

Lieutenant-Colonel Lord Brudenell's evidence.

Q. Was Captain Wathen aware that his conversation in the orderly-room was to be taken for the purpose of being recorded against him?

A. On the 4th of November, certainly not. I did not know that it would have been the case when he first came into the room; it was the consequence of his being insubordinate.

Q. At the interview, so frequently alluded to, in the orderly-room on the 8th of November, were any persons present but Sir Thomas Arbuthnot, Lord Brudenell, Captain Wathen, Captain Corkran, and Lieutenant and Adjutant Hecker?

A. Not at the first interview previous to the parade, to the best of my recollection; at the interview after the parade, Colonel Turner was present, and the quarter-master, and the captains of troops during a part of the time.

Q. Did you make any remark to the officer whose troop debt amounted to forty pounds in the month of September last; and if so, what was it?

A. I don't recollect having made any remark, because the senior major, in an official report which I now have in my hand, reported to me that the troop debts came very high, in consequence of a great number of boots and other articles furnished as the outfit for foreign service.

Q. You have stated that Major Sir Walter Scott reported to you that the troop ledgers were correct, with some trifling exceptions, previous to the inspection; ought he to have noticed the charge for the stable-jackets having been entered in Captain Wathen's troop ledger, and not in the ledger of other troops?

Lieutenant-Colonel Lord Brudenell's evidence.

A. I do not think that it was very material that he should do so: he left it most probably to the captains of troops to enter them as they please; it was an issue which had just taken place.

Q. Was the major-general ever apprised by you of any debt to so large an amount as forty pounds having existed in any troop in the 15th Hussars?

A. He was not, as the debt did not exist at the time of inspection.

Q. *By the Prisoner, through the Court.*—Was there not about thirty-one sick and lame horses at Newbridge at one time, and twenty-one cases of sore backs?

A. I have no recollection of those numbers whatever.

Q. Did you minutely inspect the squadron to which I belonged previous to its marching out of Newbridge for Carlow; and did you express much satisfaction at the manner the appointments were put on?

A. I did at six o'clock in the morning; and I never saw a squadron turn out more beautifully and regularly, or horses in better working condition.

Q. Did Major Phillips, when we were quartered at Carlow, before coming to these quarters, inform you that every horse's back in the squadron was swelled after the march; and account for it from the saddle trees not fitting, in consequence of the low condition of the horses?

A. I have no recollection of his having done so.

Q. Did I not at the same time express an opinion to that effect, and point your notice to the horses?

A. I believe Captain Wathen did.

Q. Did you not say there were so many sore backs in the squadron at Kilkenny, that it was not advisable to send the men to drill on account of it?

A. I have no recollection of having said so.

Q. On the regiment arriving in Cork for the purpose, it

was supposed, of embarkation, did I not tell you that there were many saddle-trees which, in consequence of the low condition of the horses, did not fit them, and that they could not be worked until they were altered, without wound ing the horses' backs?

Lieutenant-Colonel Lord Brudenell's evidence.

A. You may have done so.

Q. Did I not immediately give you a list of the horses whose saddle-trees did not fit?

A. You may have done so. The fitting of every saddle-tree was superintended by myself preparatory to embarkation.

Q. When you praised Captain Ives for not having so many sore-backed horses in his troop as Captain Wathen, did he not tell you that he did not wish to take credit to himself, for that he did not merit it; that he had not reported all the sore backs of his horses as Captain Wathen had done?

A. When I praised Captain Ives for his great zeal and attention to his troop, and his almost complete success in putting an end to the sore backs therein, Captain Ives said he did not wish to take too much credit to himself; but he never said that he had not reported all the sore backs of his horses, as far as I can recollect.

Q. Are there not fourteen horses at this time belonging to four troops, exclusive of mine, with broken knees?

A. Certainly not; unless you go back to at least four or five years ago.

Q. Did not the number of sore backs in my troop increase during the period of my first arrest?

A. To the best of my knowledge I should say, that there never were more than at the time you were placed under the first arrest.

[The Prosecutor closed on the first three charges.]

Lieutenant-Colonel Lord Brudenell's evidence.

First witness on the fourth charge.—Lieutenant-Colonel Lord Brudenell being already sworn, appeared in support of the fourth charge, and stated to the Court, that he received the letter now produced to the Court on the afternoon of the 12th November.

The letter was then read to the Court, of which the following is a correct copy.

" *Cork Barracks, Regimental Office,*
November 12*th,* 1833.

" My Lord,

" In accordance with your Lordship's verbal orders now given, I sit down in this office to write to your Lordship what I have just stated in your presence, and what was by your directions noted down by the adjutant; viz. that in compliance with instructions conveyed to me by the adjutant on the evening of the 8th instant, (Friday,) after the inspection, I assembled my troop after evening stables, and stated to them that I had received instructions to convey to them the entire approbation their appearance and steadiness in the field had called forth from the major-general, as well as their excellent conduct in quarters since the regiment had been under the major-general's command. I said nothing further to them that I can recollect. In reply to your Lordship's question, if I said any thing further to them on the following evening, I beg to state that I did not, or on the Sunday night after stables, or last night; but I beg voluntarily to inform your Lordship that as I did not conceive that some of the horses were so well dressed the next morning at the watering parade, as I could have wished, I took an opportunity of speaking to the men after the mid-day stables on that day; for which purpose, as soon as the stable hour was finished, I assembled them in No. 3 stable. I then stated that I had been displeased at the manner in which some of the horses had been turned out upon the morning parade; the more particularly so after the commendation which had been passed upon them by the major-general, and which they had heard expressed only the evening before; that I trusted that they would not relax in their endeavours to merit the good character that they had obtained; that I was myself very much gratified at the flattering character which had been given them by the major-general; and it had also come to my knowledge that some officers, who were present in the field, had particularly remarked upon the cleanliness and soldierlike appearance of the troop as it filed past; we were still under orders for foreign service; and if we did go, I had no doubt but that they would continue to do credit both to themselves and the regiment. I said that under all these circumstances I should excuse the drill that I had ordered, except to one man, who had spoken improperly to his non-commissioned officer.

Lieutenant-Colonel Lord Brudenell's evidence.

"I have the honour to be,
"My Lord,
"Your Lordship's
"Most obedient, humble servant,
"A. Wathen,
Captain 15th Hussars.

"*Lieutenant-Colonel Lord Brudenell,
Commanding 15th Hussars.*"

Lieutenant-Colonel Lord Brudenell's evidence.

Cross-examination.

Q. Did you not conceive your written order for the subaltern of the day to read the regimental orders, communicating the major-general's approbation of the 15th Hussars at his inspection, cancelled your verbal order for the captains and officers commanding troops on the same subject previously given by the adjutant?

A. Certainly not; the one had nothing to do with the other. The order was given to the officers commanding troops; and the regimental order was written at about the same time.

Q. Did you ascertain whether all the officers commanding troops had acted upon your verbal order?

A. I did not.

Q. Was the subaltern the orderly officer to read the orders to the troops generally?

A. He was to every troop in the barracks.

Q. Did your Lordship, between the 8th of November and the afternoon of Tuesday the 12th, inquire of me if I had made known the general's approbation to my men on the former evening?

A. I have no recollection of having spoken to you on the subject.

Q. Has your Lordship ever heard from any of the non-commissioned officers, or men of my troop, that I did make known to them at stables, on the evening of Friday the 8th of November, the orders conveyed to me by the adjutant?

A. About the 18th of last month, two non-commissioned officers of Captain Wathen's troop came forward to say, that on further consideration, they did recollect that Captain Wathen, on the evening of the 8th of November had spoken to the men of his troop in two or three of the stables relative to the major-general's approbation of the regiment, during the stable hour.

Lieutenant-Colonel Lord Brudenell's evidence.

Q. Have you not reason to believe that I was the only officer commanding a troop who communicated your verbal order to the men?

A. You did not communicate the order properly and completely. I have no reason to suppose that any other officer neglected to do so, except one, and he assigned a sufficient reason.

Q. Who was the first person to give your Lordship information about my having addressed my men?

A. It was mentioned to me accidentally and unofficially by the veterinary surgeon of the regiment.

Q. Was Lance-Serjeant Denby the first non-commissioned officer of my troop your Lordship sent for to make inquiry?

A. I believe the first to have been Serjeant-Major Thom.

Q. Did you also send for Lance-Serjeant Denby?

A. I did, in the course of the day.

Q. Had your Lordship got these men's evidence written down before you sent for me?

A. Serjeant-Major Thom's I may have probably; of Serjeant Denby I cannot give any answer.

Q. By the Court. Will your Lordship assign a specific reason for not giving an answer, respecting Serjeant Denby's evidence having been taken down?

A. Because I cannot recollect; I may have done so.

Q. You stated that you did not ascertain of the other captains commanding troops, that they had read the orders conveying the major-general's approbation to the men. What induced your Lordship to select Captain Wathen from amongst the rest for inquiry?

Lieutenant-Colonel Lord Brudenell's evidence.

A. I directed him, Captain Wathen, to write that statement, in consequence of it having been mentioned to me that Captain Wathen had addressed his troop in what I conceived a very irregular and extraordinary manner, otherwise no statement would have been called for by me.

Q. Did your Lordship or the veterinary surgeon commence the conversation relative to Captain Wathen's address to his men?

A. The veterinary surgeon.

Q. Have you ever in any other instance directed the evidence of serjeants being taken down in writing where officers were concerned; if not, what was your object in now doing so; was it with the intention of framing the present charge?

A. To the best of my recollection, to the first part of the question, certainly not. Captain Wathen's conduct, as mentioned to me, appeared very extraordinary; his conduct also on this occasion immediately occurred, after his having deliberately stated twice to the major-general, that which was contrary to truth and fact; therefore it certainly was my intention on the 12th of November, if upon inquiry I found his conduct had been improper, to report his conduct to the major-general to head-quarters.

Q. Would it not have been treating Captain Wathen fairly, if you had not communicated with some of the non-commissioned officers previous to that officer being sent for; and is your Lordship in the habit of receiving information from the non-commissioned officers against their superiors, as in the case of Captain Wathen?

A. It might have been more regular had not Captain Wathen, by his conduct on the previous Friday, in some measure justified me in treating him with less delicacy than I should have exercised towards another officer; I never before or since spoke to a non-commissioned officer relative to the conduct of any other officer.

Lieutenant-Colonel Lord Brudenell's evidence.

Q. When you ascertained that one officer had omitted to communicate your verbal order to the men, did you inquire if any more had neglected that duty?

A. No.

Second witness on the fourth charge, Lieutenant and Adjutant Hecker, of the 15th Hussars, being already sworn, was examined by Lord Brudenell.

Lieutenant and Adjutant Hecker's evidence.

Q. With reference to the fourth charge, did you convey an order from me to Captain Wathen, on Friday the 8th of November last, after the inspection?

A. Yes, I did; the purport of the verbal order was, that he was to tell his men that evening during the stable-hour, that the major-general had expressed himself gratified at the appearance and steadiness of the troops in the field that morning, and their excellent conduct in quarters.

Cross-examination.

Q. Did you communicate the same verbal order relative to the general's approbation to the other officers commanding troops?

A. Yes; with the exception of Captain Rose, as I best recollect.

Q. Are you aware whether those orders were carried into effect by those officers; if not, state if you know who did not do so, and why?

A. They were carried into effect by all except Captain Rose.

Q. Was not the orderly subaltern instructed to make

Lieutenant and Adjutant Hecker's evidence.

known the second order instead of the first, to the troops at evening stables?

A. No.

Q. Will you please to name the officers commanding troops who complied with the verbal order?

A. Captain Ives, and to the best of my belief Captain Wathen; Captain M'Queen's troop was quartered at Ballincollig, and I don't know whether the orders were mentioned to his troop by that officer.

Q. Was not Captain Wood in charge of his own troop at that time, and was it not at Cork?

A. He was not in charge of his own troop; the troop was at Cork, and it was broken up to form the other service troops.

Q. Had he not charge of the whole of his troop in all respects, except in the field?

A. Yes.

Q. Did he communicate the verbal order to his men that evening?

A. Not to my knowledge.

Q. Were the non-commissioned officers of my troop examined by the lieutenant-colonel separately, and afterwards in presence of each other, relative to my conduct?

A. Yes, separately, and not to my recollection together.

Q. Do you mean to say they have never been together, or two at a time, examined?

A. Not to my recollection.

Cross-examination finished.

Q. By the Court.—Why do you believe that Captain Wathen complied with the verbal order you gave him?

A. Because I have heard since that he did so.

Q. Who told you?

Lieutenant and Adjutant Heckers' evidence.

A. I have heard so from Serjeant-Major Thom.

Q. What reason have you for knowing some of the officers obeyed the verbal order, and be ignorant whether Captain Wood did obey it or not?

A. I heard that Captains Ives and Wathen had obeyed the order; Captain Wood, to the best of my belief, never received the order.

Q. As you communicated the order to the other officers, why did you not to Captain Wood?

A. That of Captain Wood's troop having worked in the field under Captain Wathen, I communicated the order to Captain Wathen.

Q. When did Serjeant-Major Thom tell you that Captain Wathen had complied with the order?

A. About a fortnight since.

Q. When you convey verbal orders to commanding officers of troops, are you in the habit of ascertaining if they are obeyed or not?

A. Not always.

Q. Were you desired by any one to make particular inquiries as to what officers communicated the verbal order to the troops; if so, state the nature of the directions you received, and from whom?

A. No.

Q. What was the cause for Serjeant-Major Thom informing you that Captain Wathen had obeyed the order?

A. Because he was asked by Lord Brudenell, about the time I have specified, whether he recollected Captain Wathen's having spoken to any of his men on the evening of the 8th of November.

Q. As the present charge had then been preferred, what do you suppose was his Lordship's purpose in this inquiry?

Lieutenant and Adjutant Hecker's evidence.

A. I suppose it was to ascertain from him whether Captain Wathen had spoken to his men or not.

Q. Do you mean to say that his Lordship had not previously ascertained that?

A. Serjeant-Major Thom had stated previously, that Captain Wathen had not spoken to his men, and other non-commissioned officers of his troop likewise.

Q. Were you examined, or been present, at the examination of any other witnesses, relative to the present proceedings, as to the evidence they might give?

A. No.

Q. Did not the other non-commissioned officers of Captain Wathen's troop aftérwards retract or contradict the statement they had made, in the same way as Serjeant-Major Thom?

A. Yes, one, Serjeant Clarkson.

Serjeant-Major Thom's evidence.

Third witness on the fourth charge, Serjeant-Major Thom, was recalled, and being already sworn, was examined on the fourth charge.

Q. Did Captain Wathen assemble his men after evening stables, on Friday the 8th of November last, after the inspection, to convey to them the major-general's approbation of the regiment?

A. He did not assemble them.

Q. Did he assemble them during the stable-hours on that evening, for that purpose?

A. He did not.

Cross-examination.

Q. Did you not at evening stables, on the 8th of November, tell me the orderly officer had been round, and read an order in regard to what the general had said? · Serjeant-Major Thom's evidence.

A. I told Captain Wathen that the orderly officer had read the order from the regimental orderly book to that effect.

Q. Notwithstanding what you had informed me in regard to the orderly officer, did I not speak to the men in each stable; and what did I say?

A. I cannot affirm that you did so in each stable, but can speak positively to your having done so in one; you made use of words to this effect: "I am desired to communicate to you the major-general's approbation of your discipline in the field, and good conduct in quarters.

Cross-examination finished.

Q. By the Court. Did you ever state to Lieutenant-Colonel Lord Brudenell, that Captain Wathen had not complied with the order conveyed to him relative to communicating to his troop the major-general's approbation?

A. The question put to me by Lord Brudenell was, "Did Captain Wathen assemble his troop on that evening, to communicate to the men an order delivered to him?" My answer was, that he did not do so. Lord Brudenell again sent for me, and asked me if Captain Wathen had not addressed his men in the stables on the evening of the 8th, and my answer was, he did, mentioning at the same time I was only certain of one stable.

Q. Did you ever hear that Captain Wathen did convey to the men of more than one stable, the verbal order of Lord Brudenell, respecting the major-general's approbation of the King's Hussars?

A. Yes, I have heard it from Serjeant Clarkson, and

Serjeant-Major Thom's evidence.

that he did make use of words to the same effect in the two stables of which he had the charge.

Q. How many stables did Captain Wathen's troop occupy?

A. As a service troop, the whole of six, and part of two.

Q. By the Prosecutor through the Court. Did the stable in which you heard Captain Wathen speak to his men, belong to Serjeant Clarkson's squadron?

A. It did not.

[In consequence of the indisposition of a member of the Court, the Court adjourned at three o'clock, until twelve o'clock on Monday next.]

Monday, January 6th.

Lance-Serjeant Denby's evidence.

The Court met pursuant to adjournment. Lance-Serjeant Denby, being already sworn, was examined on the fourth charge.

Q. With reference to the fourth charge, did Captain Wathen assemble the men of his troop after evening stables, on Friday the 8th of November, to convey to them the major-general's approbation of the regiment?

A. No.

Q. Did he assemble them during the stable hour that evening for the same purpose?

A. He did not.

Q. Did Captain Wathen speak to the men of your squad, during the stable hour on that evening, relative to the major-general's approbation?

A. No.

Q. How many stables had you under your charge?

A. Two.

Lance-Serjeant Denby's evidence.

Cross-examination by the Prisoner.

Q. Were you at stables during the whole stable time on the evening of the 8th of November, the day of the inspection?

A. I was.

Q. Did you tell the lieutenant-colonel you had not seen me at stables on the evening of the 8th of November?

A. Yes.

Q. Did you ever tell Serjeant Clarkson that "I had stopped your promotion, may be you would stop mine," or words to that effect?

A. No.

Q. When you give out the regimental orders, is it customary to collect the men in one stable, or give them out to them as they are assembled in each?

A. I give them out in the several stables.

Q. By the Court. Did you see Captain Wathen in the stables during any part of the evening of the 8th of November; and if so, what was he doing?

A. I did not see him.

Q. You have stated that Captain Wathen did not address the men of your squad on the evening of the 8th of November, relative to the major-general's approbation; have you since heard, and do you believe, that he did address any of the men on that evening?

A. I heard from Serjeant-Major Thom that he did address some part of the men. I do not believe it.

Q. Have you had any conversation with any person relative to this Court-Martial; and if so, state the nature of it, and with whom you had it?

A. With Serjeant-Major Thom, and Serjeant Clarkson, respecting the captains visiting the stables. Serjeant-

Lance-Serjean Denby's evidence.

Major Thom told me, that Captain Wathen had addressed some of the men in one of the troop stables, but he had no knowledge of Captain Wathen's having done it in any of the other stables; the same conversation took place with Serjeant Clarkson. I told them that I was orderly serjeant of the regiment, and had been at stables the whole of the stable hour, and that Captain Wathen had not been there that evening.

Q. You state you were at stables during the whole stable hour; were you the whole time at Captain Wathen's troop stables?

A. Yes.

Q. Did not your duty as orderly serjeant for the regiment call you to other stables besides those of the troop you belong to?

A. It did not on that evening, because the orderly serjeant for the regiment has to accompany the commanding officer in going round the stables at any time he thinks proper. I had no occasion to go round on that evening, because the commanding officer did not go round.

Q. State your stable duties as orderly serjeant, and the precise time of your attendance?

A. A quarter before seven in the morning I visit my own troop stables; at a quarter before twelve I visit my troop stables again; at a quarter before seven in the evening I do the same.

Q. Could not Captain Wathen have been in any one or more of the stables without your knowing it?

A. No.

Q. Did you on the evening of the 8th of November hear that the major-general had expressed satisfaction at the appearance and discipline of the 15th Hussars; and if so, who told you?

A. I heard the major-general's approbation read on the evening of the 8th of November, by Lieutenant Mortimer, who was orderly officer to the men of Captain Wathen's troop.

Lance-Serjeant Denby's evidence.

Q. Were you directed by any one to remain at Captain Wathen's stables that evening; and if so, by whom, and for what purpose?

A. I was not directed by any one.

Q. Have you been examined by the adjutant, or any other officer, relative to this Court-Martial?

A. Yes, by Lord Brudenell only, in the presence of the adjutant, and on one occasion Serjeant-Major Thom was present.

Q. At the time to which you allude, in a former answer, did Lieutenant Mortimer read the major-general's approbation more than once?

A. Only once to the men of Captain Wathen's troop.

Q. By the Prisoner through the Court. Did you not, as regimental orderly serjeant, accompany Lieutenant Mortimer, the orderly officer, round the stables on the 8th of November, if not, state the reason?

A. I did not, because I did not consider it the custom to follow the orderly officer round the stables, unless he wished me.

Q. By the Prisoner through the Court. State to the Court when Serjeant-Major Thom first told you that Captain Wathen had spoken to his men on the evening of the 8th of November, on the above subject.

A. About the middle of November, to the best of my knowledge.

Corporal John Alexander Mackey's evidence.

Corporal John Alexander Mackey, 15th Hussars, to the fourth charge was duly sworn and examined.

Q. Did Captain Wathen assemble the men of his troop after the evening stables, on Friday, the 8th of November last, to convey to them the major-general's approbation of the regiment?

A. No.

Q. Did he assemble them during the stable hour on that evening for the same purpose?

A. No.

Q. Did Captain Wathen speak to the men of the stable to which you belonged on that evening, relative to the major-general's approbation?

A. No.

Cross-examination.

Q. Have you not repeatedly been asked by Lieutenant-Colonel Lord Brudenell, if I was at evening stables on the 8th of November, and what answer did you give?

A. I have been repeatedly asked by Lord Brudenell; the answer I gave to Lord Brudenell was the same as I have given now, "No."

Q. Did you tell the lieutenant-colonel that your horse was not in the troop stables, but in Sir Walter Scott's, and that perhaps Captain Wathen had not been in those, or words to that effect?

A. Yes.

Q. Did Lord Brudenell say, "If you could not recollect, of course he was not there; you can take your oath he was not there," or words to that effect?

Corporal John Alexander Mackey's evidence.

A. No.

Q. State what Lord Brudenell said about it?

A. I can't remember what Lord Brudenell said about it.

Q. Did you mean to say that I was not at evening stables, or only, that you did not know whether I had been there or not?

A. Captain Wathen was not in the stable that I belonged to that evening.

Q. By the Court. Have you heard that Captain Wathen did address some of his men on the evening of the 8th of November, relative to the major-general's approbation; and if so, from whom did you hear it?

A. Yes, from private William Predmore, of Captain Wathen's troop, and in Serjeant Clarkson's squad.

Q. Had you charge of more than one stable?

A. No.

Q. Could Captain Wathen have been at the stable of his troop without your knowing it, on the evening of the 8th of November?

A. Yes.

Q. Have you been examined by any other officer besides Lord Brudenell, as to the evidence you might give to this Court, or in the presence of any other officer or man?

A. No.

Q. Could Captain Wathen have assembled the men in any stable or stables, without your knowing it?

A. No.

Q By the Prosecutor, through the Court. How many troop horses were there in the stables to which you belonged upon the evening of the 8th of November?

A. Three.

Captain G. Pitt Rose's evidence.

Witness for the Prosecution on the fourth charge, Captain G. Pitt Rose, of the 15th Hussars, was duly sworn and examined.

Q. With reference to the fourth charge, were the captains of troops ordered to attend in the regimental office on the evening of the 8th of November, after the major-general had left it?

A. They were.

Q. What occurred on that occasion?

A. Lord Brudenell ordered the captains of troops to assemble their troops, and to express to them the major-general's approbation of their conduct and appearance in the field.

Q. Did Lord Brudenell state any reason for giving the above order?

A. I do not recollect at this moment.

Q. During this interview, was the major-general's name made use of?

A. Lord Brudenell stated that it was the general's wish that it should be done.

Cross-examination.

Q. Was I present in the regimental office on the occasion to which you alluded?

A. No.

Q. Did you make known these orders to your troop; and if not, was any fault found with you for not doing so?

A. I did not make them known that evening; but subsequently Lord Brudenell asked me if I had done so; I told him I had not, and gave him a reason for not doing it, which was deemed satisfactory.

Q. Has it not long been the practice in the regiment for the officer in charge of a troop, to communicate orders or remarks similar to those made by the major-general, to the men as you find them assembled in their respective stables, if they are engaged with their horses or saddling, instead of assembling them in one body? Captain G. Pitt Rose's evidence.

A. It has been the custom, and I have constantly done it myself

Q. If you had made known to your troop the remarks of the major-general on the 8th of November, should you not have done so as you found them in their respective stables, particularly as the orderly officer had previously made them known to them, and the men had had a fatiguing day's work?

A. That depends upon the time at which I should have addressed the men; if I had spoken to them in the middle of the stable hour, I should probably have gone round to each stable, in order not to interrupt the men at their work; but if I had addressed them at the end of the stable hour, I should have addressed them at one place.

Serjeant-Major Thom being already sworn, was examined as to the fifth charge. Serjeant-Major Thom's evidence.

Q. Did Captain Wathen assemble the men of his troop at or after mid-day stables, on Saturday the 9th of November last?

A. He did after mid-day stables.

Q. State to the Court what he said to them on that occasion.

A. "I have assembled you here to tell you that I am very much pleased and gratified to hear of the satisfaction the troop gave at the inspection yesterday. I am parti-

Serjeant-Major Thom's evidence.

cularly satisfied; and it was remarked to me by a field officer of this garrison, that two gentlemen, strangers to me, had mentioned, on the left troop of the regiment passing by, not knowing whose troop it was, 'Now that is a fine troop—very soldier-like appearance.' I have no doubt, were the regiment to go on foreign service, that you would do your duty as well as any other troop in the British service. I have always found you do your duty when it was particularly required of you, notwithstanding unpleasant circumstances which have occurred. There were several horses very dirty on parade this day. I really did not expect this from you after the praise you received yesterday. I will therefore remit the punishment I ordered those men this day, with the exception of private Williams, who has otherwise committed himself, and trust it will not be the case in future."

Cross-examination.

Q. What do you consider was the cause of the men not turning out so well as usual on the watering parade on the morning after the inspection?

A. From the horses not being properly dressed after the field-day on the previous afternoon; the men being then in waiting, expecting some other parade for the major-general.

Q. Had the men leave to remain out till half-past ten the previous night; and might not that have something to do with it?

A. They had been, and it certainly might.

Q. Was there any thing unusual in my speaking to the men?

A. Nothing.

Q. How many times did the lieutenant-colonel send for you on the subject of the fifth charge?

A. Five or six times.

Serjeant-Major Thom's evidence.

Q. When was the first time, and how long did he keep you?

A. I can't state positively the time, I think the 12th of November; he kept me about a quarter of an hour.

Q. Did the lieutenant-colonel send for you alone the first time?

A. No; I went accompanied by Serjeant Denby.

Q. Were you aware that Lance-Serjeant Denby had been in the office before he came with you?

A. No, I was not.

Q. When you became aware of it, did it not appear strange to you that Serjeant Denby had not told you he had already been examined by the lieutenant-colonel?

A. I am not now aware that he had been previously examined.

Q. When you were first examined, had the lieutenant-colonel already got Serjeant Denby's list of the men I had ordered for drill?

A. I cannot say.

Q. Could the lieutenant-colonel have known the men's names except from Serjeant Denby's list?

A. No.

Q. Did the lieutenant-colonel examine you closely, and prompt you from a written statement?

A. Yes.

Q. Did the lieutenant-colonel know the names of the men on Serjeant Denby's list?

A. The lieutenant-colonel did not speak to names, but numbers.

Q. Were you informed, when you went into the office, that your words were to be taken down?

A I was.

Serjeant-Major Thom's evidence.

Q. Did you sign a statement, and when you put your name to it, did you read it, or was it read to you before you signed it?

A. I signed a statement, but I did not read it; it was read to me by the adjutant.

Q. Could you swear as to the contents of that statement being nothing but your own words?

A. No.

Q. What was said to you by Lord Brudenell when you first went to him?

A. To the best of my knowledge I was asked by Lord Brudenell if Captain Wathen had assembled the troop on Saturday the 9th of November, and to state what I had heard.

Q. At the end of your examination, did you sign a statement, or did you give a statement?

A. I signed a statement.

Q. By the Court. What did you understand by Captain Wathen's saying, "Notwithstanding the unpleasantness which had occurred?"

A. I had no idea then or since to what it related.

Serjeant W. Clarkson's evidence.

Serjeant Walter Clarkson having been already sworn, was examined on the fifth charge.

Q. Did Captain Wathen assemble the men of his troop at or after mid-day stables, on Saturday the 9th of November last; and if so, state what he said to them?

A. He did assemble them: he stated that he was very much dissatisfied with the manner in which the men had turned out that morning; but still he could not help expressing his satisfaction with the manner in which they had turned out the preceding day, and that some individuals had particularly remarked the fine and soldier-like appearance of the left troop; and if they were called upon service, he had no doubt but that it would be as good a troop as any in his Majesty's service, and that his heart was with them; under these circumstances he should overlook the punishment which he had ordered to several of the men that morning.

Serjeant W Clarkson's evidence.

Q. How many men were marked down for drill that morning by Captain Wathen's order?

A. I can't state the exact number; seven or eight.

Cross-examination.

Q. Did you ever hear Lance-Serjeant Denby make use of any words expressive of my having stopped his promotion, and his desire of revenging that supposed injury; if so, state what he said to you?

A. I have: he said to the room generally, that as Captain Wathen had stopped his promotion, he would stop Captain Wathen's.

Q. Were you present on that occasion, and was any other non-commissioned officer present?

A. I was present, and I believe there were other non-commissioned officers present; but I don't remember their names.

Lieutenant-Colonel Lord Brudenell, being already sworn, was examined to the sixth charge.

Lieutenant-Colonel Lord Brudenell's evidence.

Q. By the Judge-Advocate.—State to the Court what you know respecting the sixth charge.

A. On Tuesday, the 12th of November last, it having come to my knowledge that Captain Wathen had addressed his troop, in what I considered an irregular man-

Lieutenant-Colonel Lord Brudenell's evidence.

ner, I sent for him to the regimental office, and asked him whether he had addressed his men since the inspection; he said he had; in conformity with the order he had received from the adjutant on the preceding Friday evening, that he had expressed the major-general's approbation to them. I then said, "Did you say any thing else to them on that occasion?" he answered, "No." I then asked him, if he had assembled them on the following evening; to which he answered, "No." I then asked him if he had assembled them on the Sunday evening; to which he answered, "No." I then said, "You have stated that you said nothing to them, but expressing the major-general's approbation," or words to that effect. Before I proceed farther, I beg to state to the Court, that upon Captain Wathen's coming into the office, I told him that the adjutant would write down every thing which occurred in his presence, to prevent all mistakes afterwards. After Captain Wathen had replied to the questions put by me, which I have already stated, what was written down was read to him, and he said it was correct. After what had occurred I paused for some time. I then said, "Captain Wathen, it has come to my knowledge that you have said a great deal more to your men since the inspection, and that you have made them a sort of speech." Upon which Captain Wathen replied, "O, sir, I see the mistake under which you labour," or words to that effect. "I did assemble my troop after mid-day stables, on Saturday last;" upon which I exclaimed, "O then, Captain Wathen, you have addressed your troop again since the inspection; have the goodness to state what you said to them on that occasion." Upon which he made a statement in so hurried a manner, that I could not understand it, nor could the adjutant. I then said, "Captain Wathen, I cannot understand that—have the goodness to repeat it again." Upon which he said, "No, Sir—I decline—I shall not." I said, "that is very extraordinary; I order you to tell me what you said to your men." I believe I first of all said, "What, do you mean to say, that you will not repeat to me what you have said to your men?" He, a second time, in a very positive manner, said, "No, Sir, I shall not: I decline." After the second refusal, I paused, and then said, "Captain Wathen, this is direct disobedience of orders; but I will concede the point to you, (or words to that effect,) sit down and commit to paper what you said to your men;" which order he immediately complied with. I shortly afterwards left the office, and in about full half an hour after he had sat down, on the trumpet's sounding for parade, I returned to the office; it then appeared to me that he had been writing a great deal. I said, "Captain Wathen, I do not wish you to enter into a long statement on this subject; I only wish you to write what you said on Saturday last, when you assembled your men." I don't recollect that he gave any answer to this. I then said, "Captain Wathen, the trumpet has sounded for parade; therefore, I beg you will leave that statement in the office, and return and finish it after parade." Either on this occasion, or afterwards, I told him he might take what time he pleased to finish it. Upon which Captain Wathen got up, rolled up the paper, put it in his pocket, turned round, and said in a determined, and what I considered, very insubordinate manner—"No, Sir, I decline." Upon which, expressing my surprise, I asked him again, if he refused to obey my orders, and told him that I ordered him to leave it there; adding, about this time, that no person should read it, and that he might return afterwards to finish it. He refused again to obey

Lieutenant-Colonel Lord Brudenell's evidence.

Lieutenant-Colonel Lord Brudenell's evidence.

my orders, saying, " No, Sir, I decline—I shall not do that." Upon which I told the adjutant, to go to the parade, and bring the two senior officers upon the parade. He brought Captain Wood and Lieutenant Wakefield. I told them that Captain Wathen had refused to obey my orders. I told Captain Wathen, in their presence, that I would have my orders obeyed; that his written statement should be locked up in the chest with the regimental records before he left the room; that no person should read it, neither the adjutant nor myself—that it should be given to him immediately after he came from parade, and that he might take what time he liked to finish it, or words to that effect. He positively refused again in the same terms to obey my orders. I warned him of the consequences, and almost endeavoured to persuade him to obey my orders, by saying, " I don't wish to hurry you, reconsider the matter," or words to that effect. Shortly after, I said, " Now, Captain Wathen, what is your answer." In a positive manner, he replied, " Sir, I have already given you my answer." Upon which I desired the adjutant to go to the parade, and bring the senior field officer, as the field officer's trumpet had sounded for parade. I then narrated to him, Sir Walter Scott, all which had occurred, pointing out that Captain Wathen had repeatedly refused to obey my orders, and every thing which I have already stated, with respect to the written paper being locked up during Captain Wathen's absence at parade, in the chest, with the regimental records, to be given to him to finish when he came from parade. The senior major, Sir Walter Scott, turned to him, and said, " Captain Wathen, you are in the wrong—you must obey orders." I then paused; and on Captain Wathen neither making any reply nor showing any inclination to obey my orders, I said, " Mr. Hecker, it is now too late, it has gone on too long, (or words to that effect)—you will place Captain Wathen in arrest." I then said to the officers who were there, addressing them all—"I appeal to you all, gentlemen, whether I have not treated this officer with every possible forbearance."

Lieutenant-Colonel Lord Brudenell's evidence.

Cross-examination.

Q. With reference to the sixth charge, who gave you the information relative to my addressing my troop?

A. The veterinary surgeon.

Q. After the adjutant had called Captain Wood and Lieutenant Wakefield into the office on the 12th of November, what was your Lordship's object in sending the adjutant and myself out of the room?

A. I don't recollect sending the adjutant out of the room. I do recollect having requested you to withdraw for a few minutes—my object was to speak to the officers.

Q. What was your Lordship's object in not speaking to the officers in my presence?

A. Being on the subject of Captain Wathen's refusing to obey orders, I thought at the time it was more proper to speak to them on the subject in his absence.

Cross-examination finished.

Q. By the Court.—What was your object in putting to Captain Wathen the questions which you have mentioned to the Court?

A. Having reason to suppose that Captain Wathen had addressed his men irregularly, I considered it my duty, as commanding officer of the regiment, to make myself acquainted with what he had said to them.

Q. At the time you called Captain Wathen before you, did you contemplate putting him under arrest?

Lieutenant-Colonel Lord Brudenell's evidence.

A. I never for one moment contemplated it, and I did it most reluctantly.

Q. For what purpose did you call upon him to commit to writing what he had said to the men of his troop?

A. As an indulgence to himself, after he had two or three times refused to repeat it verbally.

Q. What induced your Lordship to order Captain Wathen to leave an unfinished statement in the office?

A. I had no object whatever in view at the time; it was not to be taken by me as a finished statement.

Q. Did it occur to you at the time, or has it since occurred to you, that Captain Wathen's declining to give the statement, might have been from his conceiving it to be intended to ground a charge against him, and thereby criminate himself?

A. It did not then, it has not since, and I cannot conceive such a thing possible, for I told him I should not read it, and that nobody else would read it.

Q. What was your reason for requiring the statement to be written in the regimental office, instead of his own quarters?

A. I had no particular reason at the time; it was an order given upon the impulse of the moment, after his refusing several times to repeat it verbally.

Q. What was your reason for requiring the statement to be left in the regimental chest?

A. So as to remove any difficulty and objection, that Captain Wathen might feel to obey my orders, as far as regarded himself.

Q. Did it never occur to your Lordship to allow Captain Wathen to remain in the office during parade, to finish his statement, or else to take it with him to parade?

A. With regard to the first part of the question, it was a parade for the reading of a regimental court-martial, and I make a point of every officer being present on those occasions. With regard to the latter part of the question, when I gave the orders, nothing of the sort occurred to me, and I expected my order to be obeyed.

Lieutenant-Colonel Lord Brudenell's evidence.

Q. Will your Lordship admit that ordering the statement to be locked up, might appear to Captain Wathen as doubting his integrity?

A. I cannot imagine any thing of the sort; because he must have known, that I did it to enable him to obey my orders, which I told him I was determined to enforce, in the manner most agreeable to his own feelings, inasmuch as the paper could not then be read by any one.

Q. Who was to have the key of the chest?

A. Really that point was not considered at the time, but no person had any right to doubt my word.

Q. Who keeps the key of the chest?

A. Generally the adjutant, who was going to the parade with myself.

Q. Had the adjutant the key of the chest on that occasion?

A. I suppose it to have been in his room.

Q. You have stated, at the time you sent for Captain Wathen, you had not contemplated putting him under arrest; are we to understand that if the present scene had not occurred in the regimental office, you would not have preferred the former five charges?

A. I have already stated that I had no intention at the time of placing Captain Wathen under arrest: if upon full inquiry into the circumstances of the case of his addressing his troop, I had considered his conduct reprehensible, I

Lieutenant-Colonel Lord Brudenell's evidence.

should have taken the opinion of the major-general on the subject. I should not have preferred the first five charges, without the approval of the major-general. I consulted and took his opinion upon the subject previous to doing so.

Q. Having previously received from the non-commissioned officers, the particulars of Captain Wathen's address to his men, do you consider it was fair to require from Captain Wathen a written statement which might afterwards be produced in evidence against him?

A. Even under the circumstances of the case, I do not consider it unfair, because I cannot conceive an officer addressing his men in such a manner that he cannot readily and instantly repeat to his commanding officer the substance of what he said on that occasion. Captain Wathen had, I conceive, shown some reluctance to tell me.

Q. State the reasons you had to suppose that Captain Wathen had addressed his men irregularly?

A. I understood that Captain Wathen had told them, that gentlemen and strangers had admired his troop particularly. I conceive that this must have alluded to civilians, and I consider it most irregular for an officer to talk to soldiers about the approbation of civilians, as to their soldierlike appearance, or appearance in the field.

Q. Do you not conceive, that all that had occurred between you and Captain Wathen was a sufficient reason for Captain Wathen to be on his guard, and disinclined to commit any thing to paper that might be brought against him?

A. It is possible to a certain extent, but I cannot conceive any disinclination superseding the necessity of an obedience to orders.

Lieutenant Colonel Lord Brudenell's evidence.

Q. When your Lordship sent for the two senior officers from the parade, had you any doubt of the legality of the order which you gave to Captain Wathen ?

A. I had not then, nor have I now, the slightest doubt of the legality of the order.

Q. Did you consult the two senior officers on the subject of Captain Wathen's alleged disobedience, or did you expect or suppose that they would interfere between your Lordship and Captain Wathen ?

A. I did not consult them ; perhaps what I said to them was wrong on the part of a commanding officer. I said to them, " You know, gentlemen, I am not a commanding officer often to give way, but I am so surprised at this positive disobedience of orders on the part of an officer, that even if I thought now I was doing any thing unfair by him, I might be disposed to concede the point ; what possible objection can Captain Wathen have to obey my orders, and leave that written statement locked up ?" They both said, " We should obey your orders, Sir ;" and one of them said, " I cannot understand Captain Wathen's objection."

Q. Did this conversation occur in Captain Wathen's presence ?

A. No, it did not.

Q. With reference to the question before the last, did you consult Major Sir Walter Scott, as senior major of the regiment ?

A. I did not ; I never consult any body but the major general of the district on any subject.

Q. Did Captain Wathen obey your orders to leave the office, readily and immediately ?

A. To the best of my recollection he did.

Q. You have stated your reason for supposing Captain

Lieutenant-Colonel Lord Brudenell's evidence.

Wathen had been irregular in his address to his troop, to have been his making reference to the approbation of civilians and strangers; how do you reconcile this with the wording of the latter part of the fifth charge, which makes the chief offence of this address to have consisted in the allusion to the recent censure your Lordship had passed on the want of attention to the care of the horses in Captain Wathen's troop?

A. I have never said that the chief offence, comprised in the fifth charge, was in the latter part of it; my former answer referred to the time when I first sent for Captain Wathen to the regimental office. I was then not thoroughly acquainted with all the bearings of the case.

Q. Was Captain Wathen apparently under any excitement when the conversation took place between you and him in the regimental office?

A. I thought his manner very extraordinary. I cannot say whether it proceeded from excitement or otherwise.

Q. Being under that impression, why did you not allow him some time to reflect upon what he had to state?

A. I know of no cause whatever for any excitement, and I thought his manner much the same as I have very often seen it on other occasions.

Q. It would appear your Lordship was desirous to get from Captain Wathen himself a statement of the terms he used, when he was addressing his troop, on the 9th of November last. Will your Lordship be pleased to state how you could, consistently, expect a correct statement from Captain Wathen, either verbal or written, at a moment when you have admitted his manner to have been most extraordinary. When three days had elapsed since he used the expressions, he never could have contemplated being called on to repeat?

A. I will state why I could, consistently, call upon him to make a statement, either verbal or written. I have already stated, that Captain Wathen's conduct was not more extraordinary on that occasion than it had been often before. I have already said that a captain of a troop is, I consider, responsible to me for any thing he may say to his men, and that I cannot understand an officer hesitating to give an answer to any question of that sort; nor can I conceive that Captain Wathen's misconduct, on the previous Friday, could possibly exempt him from giving an account to me of any supposed subsequent misconduct. Were this to be the case, it would be holding out, as it were, an indulgence to misconduct; a principle which, as commanding officer, I cannot understand.

Lieutenant-Colonel Lord Brudenell's evidence.

Q. Are the Court to understand that Captain Wathen's refusal to obey your Lordship's order, to leave his unfinished statement in the chest, was the sole cause of your Lordship's bringing these six charges against Captain Wathen; and can your Lordship state that you were not actuated by any other feelings, whether of a public or private nature, in thus bringing Captain Wathen before this tribunal?

A. I believe I have already stated, if not, I now state it, that Captain Wathen's conduct on the previous Friday and Monday, was in the hands of the major-general of the district, and was by no means finally disposed of. I can conscientiously assert, that I have been actuated by no other motive whatever, but that of the good of the service, and the welfare of the regiment which I have the honour to command. After all Captain Wathen's previous conduct, followed by a direct refusal to obey my orders, in the presence of other officers, I could not have maintained my authority as commanding officer, without referring the whole matter to head-quarters.

Lieutenant-Colonel Lord Brudenell's evidence.

Q. Has the veterinary surgeon ever before informed you of the conversations of the officers under your command; or has he in any way made you acquainted with the manner in which the officers of the 15th Hussars performed their troop duties?

A. On this occasion he mentioned it quite accidentally, and alluded to it more as a joke than any thing else. I am quite sure he had no idea there was any thing serious in the matter. I have no recollection of his having reported any officer to me; when talking of the horses and stable duties, he has often found fault with non-commissioned officers, and may occasionally have said, "The officers of such a troop are most attentive to their duties."

Q. Was the veterinary surgeon aware that you had laid charges before the major-general, when he mentioned the circumstances relating to Captain Wathen's addressing his men?

A. I have never said, or hinted, that I had laid charges against Captain Wathen at that time. I never preferred charges, or in my official letter mentioned the word charges. I received an order from Dublin to prefer charges afterwards.

Lieutenant and Adjutant Hecker's evidence.

Lieutenant and Adjutant Hecker, of the 15th Hussars, being already sworn, was recalled—examined on the sixth charge.

Q. Please to state to the Court what occurred between Captain Wathen and myself in the regimental office, on Tuesday, the 12th of November last?

A. On the 12th of November, 1833, I was in the regimental office, when Lord Brudenell asked Captain Wathen, if he had received an order conveyed through me to him, on the 8th of November. Captain Wathen said that he did, and that he had spoken to his men on that evening. Lord Brudenell then said to me, to put down on paper, questions which he would put to Captain Wathen and Captain Wathen's answers thereto; the questions were five in number, and to the following purport. 1st question was—" Was it on Friday night that you spoke to the men of your troop?" The answer was, " It was." The 2nd question was, " Did you speak to your men on Saturday night?" The answer was, " No." The 3rd question was, " What did you say to them, when you spoke to them on Friday night? Answer was, " I said that I had received orders to express to them that the major-general had been highly gratified at their appearance and steadiness in the field, and their excellent conduct in quarters, since they had been under his command." 4th question was, " Was nothing else said to them?" Answer was, " No." 5th question was, " Did you express your own individual approbation to them?" Answer was, " I did not." The above questions and answers were read over to Captain Wathen, by Lord Brudenell's orders, and he said they were correct. Captain Wathen asked Lord Brudenell if he might be informed why the above questions were put to him. Lord Brudenell replied, " I will tell you why I have done so; it has come to my knowledge this day, the 12th, that you assembled your troop on Saturday, the 9th of November, and told them that you had heard that a field officer of the garrison, as well as some strangers and civilians, had remarked that yours were a very clean and soldierlike troop at the inspection on the 18th; and that you had told them, that if they had gone on service, they would do their duty as well as any other troop; and that if they had gone, your heart would have gone with them—gone where

Lieutenant and Adjutant Hecker's evidence.

Lieutenant and Adjutant Hecker's evidence.

they would." Captain Wathen then said, that he had assembled his troop on Saturday noon, the 9th of November, and commenced saying, what he had then said to him, which Lord Brudenell told me to put on paper. I endeavoured to do so, but could not, as Captain Wathen spoke too fast for me to commit accurately to paper what he said. Lord Brudenell asked if I had done so, and I told him I had not, for the reason above stated. Lord Brudenell then told Captain Wathen to repeat what he had said on Saturday, the 9th. Captain Wathen said, that he had already mentioned what he had said to him, and declined to do so again; at the same time saying, that he would answer any communication which Lord Brudenell might choose to address to him in writing; and that he would do so in his own quarters. Lord Brudenell then told him to commit to writing what he had said, and told him it must be done in the regimental office. Captain Wathen then went to a table in the office, and commenced writing. Captain Wathen was left in the office by himself for twenty to five-and twenty minutes, when Lord Brudenell ordered me to accompany him, Lord Brudenell, to the office. Captain Wathen was still writing, and Lord Brudenell said to him, that he did not wish him to write so long a statement, but merely to put down what he had said to his troop, and that it was time for him to go to parade. Captain Wathen asked Lord Brudenell whether he was to go to parade: Lord Brudenell said, yes. Captain Wathen got up to do so, at the same time taking his statement, which he put into his pocket. Lord Brudenell told him that the statement must be left in the regimental office during his absence at parade. Captain Wathen replied, "No, sir, I decline." Lord Brudenell asked him his reasons for so doing, and Captain Wathen answered, "I do not think it right, sir." I was ordered by Lord Brudenell to bring into the office the senior officers on parade, and on their arrival Lord Brudenell explained to them the reason why they were called in, stating that he was placed in an extraordinary situation, as Captain Wathen had refused to obey his orders, telling them that he had told Captain Wathen that his written statement was to be left in the office during his absence at parade, and that nobody should read it, and that it was to be locked up in a box in which the regimental records are kept, and that I should take the key with me on parade, and that after parade the statement should be given to him, Captain Wathen, and he could finish it. Captain Wathen again declined to leave his statement; and I was ordered by Lord Brudenell to leave the office with Captain Wathen. About five minutes afterwards I was ordered to bring Captain Wathen into the office, and to request Major Sir Walter Scott to come in likewise. On their arrival, Lord Brudenell explained to Major Sir Walter Scott the reason why he had sent for him, and told Captain Wathen again to leave his statement, which Captain Wathen declined to do; I was then ordered to put him under arrest.

Lieutenant and Adjutant Hecker's evidence.

Q. When Captain Wathen said he would commit to writing what he had said to his men, how did he express himself?

A. Captain Wathen said, "I may just as well do it here," or words to that effect.

Q. State what Captain Wathen's manner was when he refused to leave the statement in the office.

A. Captain Wathen's manner was as if he had decided upon not doing so.

Lieutenant and Adjutant Hecker's evidence.

Cross-examination.

Q. Did the lieutenant-colonel, upon my first coming into the office on the 12th of November, tell me he had directed you to take down my words?

A. Not on his first arrival.

Q. During the conversation which ensued, relative to what I had said to my men, was I sent out of the office with the remark by the lieutenant-colonel, " It is very extraordinary : you may go, sir, and I'll send for you again?"

A. Captain Wathen was sent out of the office; I cannot positively state what the remark was during my absence from the office.

Q. Was regimental Serjeant-Major Collins sent for, and had that any thing to do with the present business; if so, state what passed?

A. I have no recollection of his being sent for.

Q. Was I again sent for; and did his Lordship re-examine me?

A. He was again sent for; I do not recollect any re-examination.

Q. Did not his Lordship say, " I have heard from three different sources in the regiment, you addressed your men on Saturday night?"

A. Lord Brudenell said he had heard so, but I do not recollect his having mentioned from three different sources

Q. Did Lord Brudenell ask me if I had spoken to the men on Friday evening, before or after the orderly-officer had been round; if I had spoken to them assembled in one stable, or in the separate stables; and did I say that I could not at the moment call to mind?

A. I have no recollection of that.

Q. When I declined stating over again what I had said, did I do so in a respectful and quiet manner? Lieutenant and Adjutant Hecker's evidence.

A. In a quiet manner; and as far as I could judge, respectful.

Q. Did his Lordship approach me to take the paper I was writing, and say; "It's time for parade, give it to me?"

A. Lord Brudenell did not approach Captain Wathen; but he told him it was time for him to go to parade; he did not say, "Give the paper to me," according to the best of my recollection.

Q. Do you know the reason of Lord Brudenell's anxiety to possess himself of my unfinished, uncopied statement?

A. Not in the least.

Q. Do you conceive my declining to leave the paper I had been writing, was done with a view to show disrespect to Lord Brudenell, or only that I did not consider it right that I should be deprived of an unfinished document, which might hereafter be brought against me?

A. Captain Wathen's first declining to leave the statement, I did conceive that he considered it right to keep his unfinished statement; but after Lord Brudenell had explained to him that nobody should read the paper, and that it should be given to him after parade to finish, I did then conceive, that Captain Wathen's refusal arose from disrespect to Lord Brudenell.

Q. You said on a former occasion, that you never received instructions to take down in writing particular officers' statements; how do you reconcile this with what you have now said, that you were ordered to take down my words on this occasion?

A. Lord Brudenell gave me that order in presence of Captain Wathen, Lord Brudenell putting the questions,

Lieutenant and Adjutant Hecker's evidence.

and Captain Wathen giving the answers. The only reason which I can suppose that Lord Brudenell wished on this particular occasion to have taken down Captain Wathen's answers to his questions was, to ascertain whether they agreed with what the non-commissioned officer had previously stated to him.

Q. Did you upon all occasions of taking down the words and manner of the officers, when in conversation with his Lordship, take down the words and manner of the lieutenant-colonel, and did you ever alter or revise any of the statements taken down by you?

A. On those occasions on which I have taken down conversations, I have perhaps more fully taken down the words and manner of Lord Brudenell than the officer, and have no recollection, with one exception, of revising or altering what I had originally put down.

Q. Do you know, or can you imagine, from what source the lieutenant-colonel derived his information, that I had addressed my men?

A. I only learned a few days ago that it was from veterinary-surgeon Hograve that Lord Brudenell first heard it.

Q. Do you think Serjeant Denby was the first non-commissioned officer sent for, or who came, in regard to the subject?

A. To the best of my recollection, Serjeant Denby was the first sent for, and came first.

Q. Had Serjeant Denby a written statement, or did he sign a statement drawn up by you, or both?

A. Serjeant Denby had no written statement, to my knowledge, when he came to the office on the 12th. The statement which I committed to paper by Lord Brudenell's order, of what Serjeant Denby stated, was not, to the best of my recollection, signed by that non-commissioned officer till after Captain Wathen's arrest.

Lieutenant and Adjutant Hecker's evidence.

Q. Did he give at any time a written statement?

A. No.

Cros-examination finished.

Q. *By the Court.*—When Lord Brudenell spoke to Captain Wathen in the regimental office, on Tuesday the 12th of November last, did he address him in his ordinary tone of voice, or in a manner that implied displeasure?

A. In his ordinary tone of voice.

Q. Did Captain Wathen appear flurried, or in a state of excitement, while the conversation took place between Lord Brudenell and him in the regimental office; and if so, have you often seen him in the same state?

A. Captain Wathen did appear to me to be excited; I do not recollect ever having seen him so much so.

Q. Have you never found a similar difficulty in taking down conversations in the orderly-room, to that you have stated on the present occasion?

A. Yes; I have occasionally found the same difficulty.

Q. Has Lord Brudenell always acted on the substance of what you have taken down?

A. No; not always.

Q. *Through the Court, by the Prosecutor.*—With reference to former evidence, did I ever assign any reason to you, in the presence of Captain Wathen, for ordering what Captain Wathen said on the 12th of November to be committed to writing?

A. Not to my recollection.

Q. You have stated that you revised something which was once taken down; please to state what it was, and by whose order?

Lieutenant and Adjutant Hecker's evidence.

A. It was as to the manner of an officer, and by Lord Brudenell's order.

Lieutenant Edward Wakefield's evidence.

Lieutenant Edward Wakefield, of the 15th Hussars, was duly sworn and examined on the sixth charge.

Q. Please to state to the Court what occurred between Captain Wathen and myself in the regimental office, on Tuesday the 12th of November last, and who was present?

A. I was desired by the adjutant to attend in the orderly-room. On going there I found Lieutenant-Colonel Lord Brudenell and Captain Wathen; the adjutant and Captain Wood were also present. Lord Brudenell said that an officer had positively refused to obey his orders. Lord Brudenell addressed himself to Captain Wood and myself in the following words, as nearly as I can remember: that he had permitted Captain Wathen to put down in writing an address which he had made to the men of his troop some time previous. Captain Wathen had refused to repeat this statement verbally, which he had been called upon to do. In consequence of his speaking so quickly, that the adjutant could not take it down in writing, that Captain Wathen proceeded to write out the statement; before he had finished the statement that he was writing out, the time had arrived for Captain Wathen's presence at parade, and Lord Brudenell wished Captain Wathen to leave the statement in the office, which Captain Wathen declined doing. Lord Brudenell then said that the written statement should not be read by any one; should be given up to the adjutant to be locked up by him in a box in the orderly-room, and returned to Captain Wathen after parade. Captain Wathen respectfully declined giving it up.

His Lordship repeated the same thing more than once in my presence to that effect. After Captain Wathen declined giving up the statement he retired from the office, and some time afterwards he was recalled. In addition to the persons whom I have mentioned, Major Sir Walter Scott was present. A similar statement was made by Lord Brudenell to Sir Walter Scott, who said he did not see any impropriety in the address being locked up. Captain Wathen declined leaving it, and he was placed in arrest. Sir Walter Scott then said, that if Captain Wathen considered for a moment, that he would see the propriety of acquiescing with Lord Brudenell's orders. His Lordship said, it was too late; and Lord Brudenell also said, that any honest man must say that he had behaved with great temper; or words to that effect.

Lieutenant Edward Wakefield's evidence.

Q. Did not Lord Brudenell say to you, "I in the first instance asked Captain Wathen to give it to me; but I afterwards consented to his leaving it in the office in a box?"

A. I remember words to that effect.

Major Sir Walter Scott, of the 15th Hussars, was duly sworn and examined as to the sixth charge.

Major Sir Walter Scott's evidence.

Q Please state to the Court what occurred between Captain Wathen and myself in the regimental office, on Monday the 12th of November last, when you were present.

A. I was in the regimental office on the 12th of November, and then heard Captain Wathen positively decline to give up a written statement, when ordered to do so by Lord Brudenell; and although Lord Brudenell told him that such statement would not be read by him or the adjutant,

Major Sir Walter Scott's evidence.

but should be locked up in a box in the office, and delivered to him after parade. On Captain Wathen's declining to give up this statement, Lord Brudenell asked me if I saw any reason why he should not do so. I said, "No; I see no reason why he should not." Lord Brudenell then ordered Captain Wathen under arrest; on which I said, "My Lord, I am sure Captain Wathen, on consideration, and under these circumstances," meaning that the statement should be given back after parade, "will see the propriety of giving up the statement." Lord Brudenell said, "No, no, it is too late; I appeal to any honest man if I have not had ample forbearance, or sufficient temper," or words to that import. I turned to Captain Wathen, and said, "You had better give up the statement." Captain Wathen said, "No, sir, as it is now too late." Lord Brudenell, in the mean time, took up his cap and was leaving the office, which he quitted immediately. Captain Wathen's declining to obey the order was done in a perfectly respectful manner, and with a low tone; and the order was given firmly and decidedly, and temperately also.

[It being four o'clock, the Court adjourned until eleven o'clock the following morning.]

Thursday, January 9.

The Court met pursuant to adjournment.—Major Mitchell was still absent from indisposition.

The examination of Major Sir Walter Scott was resumed.

Cross-examined by the Prisoner.

Q. When Lord Brudenell told you, on the 12th of November, that I disobeyed orders, did you at the moment consider whether it was, as expressed by the articles of war, a lawful command, and what is now your opinion?

Major Sir Walter Scott's evidence.

A. I did not at the moment consider whether it was lawful or unlawful; but the same day I thought that the command was not a lawful one.

Q. Was I not placed in arrest before I had time to benefit by your advice, had I been so disposed; and did it appear, from his Lordship's hasty manner, as if he willingly seized upon an opportunity to place me under arrest?

A. With regard to the first part of the question, yes; to the latter part of the question, yes; as he allowed no time for consideration on my suggestion.

Q. Did you make use of these words to me in the regimental office, when appealed to by Lord Brudenell, "Captain Wathen, you are in the wrong; you must obey orders;" if not, state what you did say?

A. My words were, "Surely, Captain Wathen, you may give up the statement."

Q. Was my conduct towards his Lordship on the occasion in question perfectly respectful, and have you not always observed it to be such?

A. Captain Wathen's conduct was very respectful, and before me has been invariably such on all occasions.

Q. Do you consider that I thwarted and opposed Lord Brudenell; or, on the contrary, that upon principle, and with a view to the good of the regiment, I paid that deference to his Lordship which his situation demanded?

A. I do not consider that you ever opposed or thwarted Lord Brudenell as commanding officer of the regiment; Captain Wathen has always paid due deference to him, and I am sure has nothing but the good of the regiment at heart.

Major Sir Walter Scott's evidence.

Q. Were you put upon the duty of president of a regimental court-martial, on Monday the 11th of November; and if so, state why you were put upon such an unusual duty?

A. I was; and on asking Lord Brudenell on Saturday the 9th, how it was that I should sit upon a regimental court-martial, as there were captains present with the regiment to do that duty, Lord Brudenell said he could not put Captain Wathen on that duty; he could not trust him, or words to that effect, after his conduct the night before in the presence of the major-general. This conversation was not confidential.

Q. Did you consider that I was then unfit for any regimental duty?

A. I did not see you on Saturday till late in the day, when I saw nothing in your manner to render you unfit for any regimental duty.

Q. Have you remarked that Lord Brudenell has lately been harsh towards me, particularly since the reading of Lord Hill's decision, that the former charges against me were to be given up?

A. Once in the field, and after reading Lord Hill's letter, you were released from arrest in what I consider a most ungracious manner.

Q. Pray state to the Court what his Lordship's observations were when he had read this letter.

A. "This letter, which must be considered decisive upon what Lord Hill is pleased to term my differences with Captain Wathen, admits of no comment; but I must say, Lord Hill has been misled in his opinion with regard to the adjutant, as it is my opinion that the adjutant fully and adequately performed his duty; and at the approaching inspection he would write such a letter to the major-general, as would induce him, in his confidential report, to make such representations, as would do away with any impression at head-quarters of the adjutant's want of zeal; that he was certain Captain Wathen had had half an hour's notice, or at least twenty minutes." This took place before the officers in the mess-room assembled there by Lord Brudenell.

Major Sir Walter Scott's evidence.

Q. Do you not consider that the discovery lately made of the conversations being taken down in the orderly-room has been most painful and revolting to the feelings of the officers?

A. There can be no doubt but that it has been both.

Cross-examination finished.

Q. By the Court.—Do you now imagine, that if Lord Brudenell had not quitted the office so suddenly, when saying, "It is too late," that there would have been a probability of arranging the affair between Lord Brudenell and Captain Wathen without an appeal to a court-martial?

A. I knew not Captain Wathen's motives for refusing.

Q. From every thing that has come under your observations as major of the 15th Hussars, what do you consider Captain Wathen's general conduct to have been as a duty officer, and towards his superiors?

A. Captain Wathen has, in my opinion, been always a zealous duty officer, and respectful towards his superiors.

Q. It has been stated to the Court, that a great many horses in Captain Wathen's troop had sore backs; do you attribute these sore backs in any degree to the carelessness or neglect of Captain Wathen; or if not, to what cause?

A. From no neglect on Captain Wathen's part; but

Major Sir Walter Scott's evidence.

they arose, in my opinion, partly from the thin and bad condition of the horses, owing to which the saddle-trees did not fit as they ought to have done; and also to long drill, when the men could not ride so steadily and well at the termination of the field day as at other times if the drill had been shorter.

Q. Are you aware whether Captain Wathen informed the lieutenant-colonel, " if the saddle-trees were not altered, the horses of his troop must have sore backs?"

A. I have heard Captain Wathen say that he had spoken to the lieutenant-colonel on that subject.

Q. You have said Captain Wathen was released from arrest in what you consider a most ungracious manner; pray relate the language which referred to Captain Wathen, and Lord Brudenell's manner towards that officer?

A. Lord Brudenell asserting any thing with regard to the adjutant having performed his duty correctly, was as much as saying that he, Captain Wathen, had not performed his. The manner in which he said, " Release that officer from arrest;" on his leaving the room, both his look and gestures were ungracious.

Q. Has any thing come under your observation to make you think that Captain Wathen, from having been once placed in arrest before by Lord Brudenell, had become even more careful than before to avoid giving any cause of offence towards Lord Brudenell?

A. I do not recollect.

Q. By Lord Brudenell, through the Court.—At the time you have asserted that my look and gesture were ungracious, was it not so dark I could scarcely see to read?

A. There being light enough to see to read, there was of course light enough to see any gesture of his Lordship.

Q. Did I not tell the officers that I was authorized by the major-general to say something relative to the adjutant?

Major Sir Walter Scott's evidence.

A. I do not recollect Lord Brudenell saying so; the remarks were made as if from himself.

Q. How do you account for there having been only one sore-backed horse in Captain Blyth's troop, and twenty-three in Captain Wathen's troop, both troops having performed the same duties?

A. I do not know such to be the case.

Q. Were not the saddle-trees in Captain Wathen's troop altered and fitted by me, and were there not as many or more sore backs afterwards?

A. The saddle-trees were altered at the same time when those of the other troops were altered; but I cannot say any thing to the extent of this evil, either before or afterwards.

Q. Will you state to the Court whether you do not consider conversations between yourself as senior major, and myself as commanding officer, with regard to junior officers, as confidential?

[This question was considered objectionable by the Court. His Lordship having pressed its being put, the Court was cleared, and on its being re-opened, his Lordship was informed that the Court had decided that the question should not be put.]

Q. Was it your own opinion that my order was unlawful, or was it suggested to you by any body, and by whom?

A. My own opinion, on consideration, and further strengthened by conversation with other officers; so much so, that in his Lordship's room, when he gave me the charges to read after they were approved, I observed that it was a case for the judge-advocate-general in point of law.

Major Sir Walter Scott's evidence.

Q. By the Court.—Has Lord Brudenell been in the habit of communicating to you, or consulting you as senior major of the regiment, on all matters relative to the discipline of the corps, and the conduct of the officers; or have you ever had any confidential conversation with his Lordship regarding either?

A. No; I can recollect no occasion upon which I have been consulted.

The case then closed for the prosecution; Captain Wathen requested that the Court would give him until Monday next to prepare his defence.

The Court acceded to his request, and adjourned to that day at twelve o'clock.

Monday, January 13.

The Court met at twelve o'clock pursuant to adjournment.

Captain Wathen's defence.

The Prisoner entered upon his defence, and addressed the Court as follows:—

"Mr. President and Gentlemen,

"It must always be considered a misfortune for an officer, that his conduct should, at any period, have been brought under the consideration of a court-martial; as even in the event of his being honourably acquitted, it must still remain a disadvantageous circumstance to him throughout his military career. In ordinary courts-martial the particulars of the case are soon lost sight of, if indeed they are ever generally known; but, however this may be, it is never forgotten, that such an officer *was* brought to trial, and the conclusion is naturally made, that so serious a measure was not resorted to. without sufficient, or at least, apparently reasonable, grounds. Captain Wathen's defence.

"Unfortunately for myself, this is now the second time, within the short period of a month, that charges have been preferred against me. Upon the first occasion, I was influenced by reflections such as I have described; but it has at length become impossible to avoid recourse being had to so disagreeable an alternative. I deeply lament that circumstances should ever have arisen, which render such a course necessary, and I feel that I have had no share in creating them; but as the necessity *does exist*, I am not only ready to meet the charges preferred against me, but I feel grateful to the General commanding-in-chief, and to the Lieutenant-General commanding in this country, for having thus afforded me an opportunity of endeavouring to clear myself from the representations, which have been put forth to my discredit, by Lieutenant-Colonel Lord Brudenell. In the defence, upon which I am about to enter, I am aware that opportunities will present themselves, of which I might with facility avail myself, to gratify vindictive feelings, were I so disposed; but I must now declare, that notwithstanding the injuries and persecutions I may have received, I neither am, or ever have been, actuated by such motives. In vindicating my own character, it is not my wish to misrepresent or colour facts, but to observe a strict regard to truth. My object is to prove myself innocent, and my wish, to be restored to my duties, without a stain upon my character.

"The charges which are preferred against me by his Lordship are of a very serious nature. I am not only charged with conduct unbecoming an officer and a gentleman, in making false statements, and in having spoken and written untruths, but also with disobedience of orders,

Captain Wathen's defence.

which, as a soldier, is one of the greatest crimes of which I could have been guilty. The charges preferred against me are six in number. I could have hoped, that standing in the position that I now unfortunately do, under the shelterof this honourable Court, no further attacks would have been made upon my character; but the prosecutor, in the commencement of his address, has brought a seventh charge against me; that of intriguing with the public press. Mr. President and Gentlemen, I repel the insinuation. On the honour of a soldier, I am totally unacquainted with the source from whence the papers have derived their information. I have never, either directly or indirectly, influenced the press; or had any knowledge of the manner in which the paragraphs alluded to found their way into the English and Irish newspapers; and I beg also to make a similar disavowal of any knowledge of the circumstance, on the part of my immediate friends. His Lordship uses the word *party:* this inference rests solely with his Lordship. He says that a garbled statement was presented to the public, of a conversation which took place in the orderly-room, when only his Lordship, the adjutant, and myself, were present. His Lordship had placed me in arrest; my friends inquired the reason,—my conscience was clear, I therefore observed no secresy on the subject. Was there any reason that I should have done so? Beyond this, I gave no publicity to what had taken place; I felt assured, that, in the event of my being brought to trial, justice would take its course. Officers and gentlemen could not, by possibility, permit themselves to be influenced by ex-parte statements, and I well knew, that *evidence* only, which should be produced before the Court, could assist my cause, or insure me an acquittal.

"I feel that I have not merited the unkindness which I

have met with at the hands of the prosecutor; but as, through his Lordship's means, I am now placed in the painful situation of a prisoner before this honourable Court, it is a source of satisfaction to me to know that the circumstances of the case are submitted to the consideration of officers, in whose judgment and integrity I have reason to place the most confident reliance; and as my conduct is under the investigation of a court of equity and honour, I have not deemed it necessary to avail myself of any legal assistance whatever.

Captain Wathen's defence.

"There are two circumstances connected with the charges now before the Court, which will not escape their notice, and which cannot but create surprise. What I allude to is as follows. The immediate cause of my being placed under arrest, is not made the *first* and *principal* charge against me, but is the last in the list; and although it contains an accusation of disobedience of orders, it has been but lightly dwelt upon in the prosecution. The next inconsistency, to which I wish to direct the attention of the Court, is, that no intimation has hitherto been made to me by the prosecutor, in regard to the matter and accusation contained in the fourth charge. I am therein accused of conduct unbecoming an officer and a gentleman, in having made a statement contrary to truth and fact; but not one word was said to me by his Lordship at the time of, or since, my arrest, that could lead me to suppose that he entertained such an opinion of my statement as he has now declared to have been the case. I could, at the time, have as easily explained the circumstances to his Lordship, as I can upon the *present occasion,* to the members of this honourable Court; indeed, with much greater facility, as it is necessary that I should not only detail, but substantiate, events, which in the first instance, and with regard to his Lordship, would have been unnecessary. At all hazards, the Lieutenant-colonel appears to have been determined to prefer charges against me.

"I was placed under arrest on a charge of what his Lordship was pleased to term disobedience of orders, in not delivering up into his possession an unfinished, unrevised, and uncopied letter. This was the specific charge alleged against me; at that time the other charges, as has already been shown, related to antecedent circumstances, which had passed over without any intimation being made to me that a complaint was to be formed upon them, and I therefore had every reason to suppose, when placed under arrest, that the cause of that circumstance would be considered my chief or only offence. It may have been prudent, on the part of the prosecution, to avoid making the cause of my being placed under arrest a conspicuous charge; but, as far as I am concerned, there is no reason that I should be influenced by similar motives. I have always endeavoured to do my duty in an upright manner, and I have therefore no cause to evade inquiry. On the contrary, I now court investigation: it affects my character that every circumstance should be seen into, and it is necessary to my defence and exculpation, that instead of slurring over any part of the transactions, (more particularly with regard to my arrest,) that I should put the Court in possession of every circumstance relating to it, not only at the moment of the arrest taking place, but with regard to the events which led to it. This information will enable the Court to judge whether or not the situation in which I was placed with regard to the Lieutenant-colonel, was such as to render the document or letter, mentioned in the sixth charge, of such importance to me as to warrant my concluding that it was but common prudence on my part not to deliver it up, until I had well considered the words set down in it; and whether, from what had gone before, I had reason to fear, that if I neglected this precaution, that advantage might not be taken of it to my own detriment. It is probable that the Court, without any defence, would acquit me of the charge of disobedience of orders; but it is also essential to me to clear myself from any blame, which might attach to me, from an apparent unwillingness and obstinacy, in refusing to accede to the wishes of my commanding officer; and this can only be accounted for, and made apparent to the Court, by their being informed by me of the previous connecting events, which caused me to be thus suspicious, and influenced my conduct *upon that occasion and others* mentioned in the charges. It will therefore be necessary to give a summary of what has passed, in connexion with the charges now before the Court, from the period of my being released from former arrest, by command of the General Commanding-in-Chief, Lord Hill, as it was from that moment that the disposition was evinced on the part of his Lordship, which ultimately led to my being placed in my present trying position. On Sunday, the 20th of October, the officers having been assembled in the mess-room, by order of Lieutenant-Colonel Lord Brudenell, his Lordship then read the decision of Lord Hill, relative to the charges which had previously been preferred against me. Lord Brudenell then commented at some length on it, stating that the General Commanding-in-Chief must have decided on some points under a wrong impression. He brought again into notice the past transaction, which it had been the object of Lord Hill to bury in oblivion, through his commands, expressed in the letter which Lord Brudenell was still holding in his hand. The Lieutenant-colonel having finished his comments upon

Captain Wathen's defence.

Captain Wathen's defence.

Lord Hill's decision, and his remarks upon my own conduct, which I considered to be fresh cause of offence, said to the adjutant in a peculiarly ungracious manner, 'In consequence of this decision of Lord Hill's, release that officer from arrest.'

"This last observation the Lieutenant-colonel accompanied by a supercilious wave of the hand, and left the room. Could I have hoped that his Lordship's future conduct towards me would have been in any manner conciliatory, or even forbearing, I should have returned to my duties with pleasure, and have felt gratified at the termination which had been put to a very unpleasant transaction; but from what I had just witnessed, and from previous occurrences which had taken place, I had reason to fear, that for the future it would be both difficult and dangerous for me to serve under his Lordship's command. I therefore wrote to his Lordship, requesting that he would apply to the major-general to grant me leave of absence to proceed to England, intending to consult with my friends in what manner to relieve myself from the embarrassing position in which I conceived I was placed. His Lordship, in reply, demanded of me, through the adjutant, what *were* the urgent *private* affairs which would call me away previous to the inspection of the regiment. I replied, I was desirous of leave to go to England upon matters immediately affecting my future prospects: that it was of the utmost importance to me, (which was absolutely the case,) to see a relation, before he quitted London for the winter, and that it was therefore an object to me, to get away by the next packet. I received the following answer in reply:—

Captain Wathen's defence.

"*Cork Barracks, Oct.* 20, 1833.

"Sir,

"I am directed by Lieutenant-Colonel Lord Brudenell to inform you, in the most decided manner, that he will not consent to apply for leave of absence for you; his objections are as follow:—

"1st. He does not think the day on which an officer's conduct is animadverted on in strong terms, by order of the general commanding in chief, is the proper moment for him to apply for the indulgence of leave of absence.

"2ndly. Lieutenant-Colonel Lord Brudenell does not consider your troop in good order, although the attention of the troop officers within the last month has effected considerable improvement in it. The lieutenant-colonel considers that your troop, now fifty-four horses strong, requires the constant care and attention of all its officers.

"'I have, &c.

(Signed) "C. H. J. Hecker.

"Lieutenant and Adjutant 15th King's Hussars.

"*To Captain Wathen, 15th King's Hussars.*

"I think it will be apparent from the tenor of the letter I have just read, that his Lordship did not entertain any favourable disposition towards me. The reference contained in it to Lord Hill's letter, appeared to me to be in direct opposition to the spirit of the instructions conveyed to Lieutenant-Colonel Lord Brudenell in that document. I feel certain, that it never was the intention of the general commanding-in-chief, that his decision, which he positively enjoined must be considered final, should be made available as a subject of after reproach. Neither could I bring

Captain Wathen's defence.

to my recollection any passage in the letter, from which it might be inferred that it had been intended to convey to me such reproof as was implied by the lieutenant-colonel.

" The next objection to my obtaining leave of absence was, that my troop was out of order, but beyond general blame, his Lordship was unable to point out in what respect it differed from others; and at the half-yearly inspection, which took place shortly afterwards, the major-general did not express any wish of excluding my troop from the share of praise which he was pleased to bestow upon the regiment generally, the condition of which, he said, he had probed to the bottom, and could not find a fault. His Lordship states that my troop had improved under the management of my subalterns, during the month I was absent, viz. during the time I had been kept under arrest. I can only aver, that my most zealous and unremitting attention had always been devoted to it, and although I had reason to be satisfied with the manner in which the duties were discharged by my subaltern officers, I am quite sure that they do not themselves consider that they either did, or were able, to manage it better than I had done. The lieutenant-colonel next states, that my troop being fifty-four horses strong, requires the constant care and attention of all its officers; but what are the steps taken by his Lordship? Lieutenant Wood obtained promotion in the regiment, consequently I was deprived of his service in the troop; but notwithstanding this circumstance, his Lordship immediately granted leave of absence to the other officer, Lieutenant Hickman, so that I was altogether without a subaltern.

" I might also remark, that as the service squadrons still continued formed, all the troops were equally strong with mine; and although I believe my turn for leave was first, Captain Macqueen and Captain Ives were allowed to go away after the inspection, and I was detained. On my being again placed under arrest, his Lordship put a very junior lieutenant in the regiment in command of the troop, which his Lordship had repeatedly informed me, was not only in the worst order in the regiment, but even in the service. On the first field day after my release from arrest, the unkindness of his Lordship was again apparent. Being in the command of a squadron, I occasionally pointed with my sword towards the men in the ranks, and I made those signals with it which are customary. At these times, and always during some manœuvre which required my attention, his Lordship would desire me to carry my sword, although it was not the custom to do so, and say in a vexatious manner, 'Carry your sword, sir; can't you carry your sword properly?' This observation he made to me frequently, as also remarks upon my riding, and method of holding my reins. On the 4th of November, the troops were again at exercise, in a field near the barracks; I had not gone through the parade movements since my release from arrest; the regiment trotted past in open column of *troops*. I inadvertently placed myself in front of the centre of my troop, which had formerly been the order under Sir Hussey Vivian. I was occupied about the interval, and forgetting myself, I made this mistake. The lieutenant-colonel allowed the troop to pass; he then halted the regiment, and, riding to the centre, addressed me reproachfully, and so loudly, that every one in the field might hear; his Lordship stated, that if I could not command my troop after all this time, he would bring up the junior cornet in the regiment to take the command of it; that this captain had been six years, (I had been seven,) a captain

Captain Wathen's defence.

Captain Wathen's defence.

in this regiment, and could not even now trot past in his place. His Lordship made many other observations to the same purport. I of course made no reply, but I subsequently learnt, that at a field day immediately previous, another officer mechanically made the same mistake, which had been also noticed by his Lordship, but not in so angry and reproachful a manner as he had used towards myself. On the afternoon of the day on which his Lordship had found fault with me in so extraordinary a manner in the field, (the 4th of November,) as I was superintending the stable duties afterwards, the adjutant came to me and said, 'The colonel wants you and Surret, (a private in my troop,) in the office directly. He is to come in his stable-jacket without waiting. (May I request the particular attention of the court to this circumstance?) I accordingly went with the man into the office. The lieutenant-colonel asked private William Surret what was the reason he did not sign his accounts. The man stated his reasons, and still declined to sign the ledger. The lieutenant-colonel spoke at considerable length, inducing an argument on the part of the private, as to the propriety of his having been sent to drill, in which, however, I took no part, although I had made intercession for him upon the subject in question on a former occasion. His Lordship told him he was one of those lazy, idle fellows of this troop, (meaning my troop,) that there was not such another troop in the service; that if he had done his duty, he should have reported it as inefficient at head quarters. His Lordship then dwelt for some time upon the demerits of my troop. The lieutenant-colonel continued, addressing the man, 'Do you choose to sign your account, sir? Now, I'll have you out before all the regiment; I won't wait for you to complain to the general, but I'll have you out—you shall complain—I'll force you—I'll oblige you to do so; if you were to go back for fifty years, such a troop could not be found throughout the service.' I need not, I am sure, appeal to this honourable tribunal, what effect such remarks, made to a private of my troop, were likely to produce among the men, to whom that private naturally would relate them, and that at a time, when, if his Lordship's observations were just, it required the authority of the captain to be more particularly upheld, for the improvement of the troop. I made no observations till the private left the office. I then said, 'Your Lordship has made very severe animadversions upon my troop. After what you have said, and that in the presence of a private, I think it will be but justice to me that you should bring the state of it under the notice of the General at the inspection, and then make good the assertions you have put forth.' His Lordship replied, 'I shall do as I please; you are not to dictate to me, Sir.' I was then allowed to withdraw, but was soon recalled. Lord Brudenell said, in a most imperious tone, 'You addressed me in an improper manner, Sir, when you were here just now. Now, Sir, what do you mean by what you said?' I replied, 'My lord, I am not aware I said any thing improper.' 'Yes, you did; do you *dare* to doubt my word, Sir? This is what you said,' and his Lordship *took up a written paper*. Although I had been so prepared by events which preceded, not to be much surprised at any mode of proceeding that might be adopted in regard to myself, I confess I was astonished and shocked at what I now witnessed. My words had been clandestinely taken down in writing, without giving me any reason to suspect that such a proceeding might be in contemplation, and without any occurrence having taken place

Captain Wathen's defence.

Captain Wathen's defence.

that could in any manner form a pretext for such an unheard of transaction between officer and officer.

"I, therefore, saw the necessity of being particularly on my guard; and notwithstanding the feelings which the discovery of such a circumstance might naturally be supposed to have excited in the mind of any man, who had received the education of a gentleman, I did not give utterance to any angry expressions; I merely declined reading the paper; and in reply to the singularly violent manner in which his Lordship demanded of me, if I doubted his word? if I meant to deny that those were my words? I replied, that I was not aware that my words had been taken down in writing. His Lordship rejoined, 'I dare say not, Sir! but I find it very convenient!! Do you mean to deny that these were your words?' As I observed that the adjutant was still taking down my words, I said, 'Under these circumstances, I think it better not to say any thing further, than that I am not aware of having said any thing improper.' 'Then, Sir,' replied the lieutenant-colonel, 'I tell you that you did; and I now reprimand you for it. I desire you to be more careful for the future. I can tell you, that in regard to your troop, I shall adopt any course I think fit; I shall not, in order to *gratify your feelings*, report it to the general. I sha'n't do any such thing, but you may adopt any course you please.' I was retiring—his Lordship pointed with his finger to the floor at his feet, and said, 'Come back, Sir.' I waited, and said, 'Has your Lordship any further commands?' 'No; you may retire.' It is material to my defence, to show that I had grounds to feel doubtful as to the fairness of the intentions of the lieutenant-colonel in regard to me, and I therefore solicit the Court to allow their attention to dwell upon the circumstances I have just related, and upon a consideration of them to decide, whether or not I was justified in forming the conclusion I at that moment came to, and which materially influenced my conduct on a subsequent occasion—namely, that the lieutenant-colonel was seeking occasion to place me in the wrong.

Captain Wathen's defence.

"I think that from this time his Lordship must have perceived, from my reluctance to enter into any discussions, that I had determined to endeavour not to be led into error by any reproach, however unmerited; but he still did not abstain from making remarks upon my troop, and upon my management of it, which he well knew would be most hurtful to my feelings; and which it must have been apparent to him, was a course most likely to induce an officer to give hasty, or intemperate replies. Accordingly, at parades, his Lordship invariably found fault; I could not, myself, see the occasion, but it was of course for the commanding officer to judge of such matters, and I offered no excuses. The senior major was generally present, and I shall hereafter request his opinion as to whether my troop appeared to be dirty or improperly turned out, and whether he considers that there was any foundation for its being called the worst in the regiment, and in the service. I must entreat the particular attention of the Court to what I have now to relate. On the *seventh* of November, the day previous to that on which the regiment was to be inspected by Major-General Sir Thomas Arbuthnot, Lieutenant-Colonel Lord Brudenell sent for me into the office. After making some remarks upon my books, his Lordship said to me, that my debt was very great, that it was greater than that of any other troop in the regiment, and *that I should have to account for it to the major-general at the inspection next day.* I replied, that

Captain Wathen's defence.

I was aware my debt was great, but that I had reason to believe, that it was not in reality greater than that of other troops. His Lordship said, 'But I tell you it is,' and referred to another troop debt much lower than mine. I said that I was responsible only for my own debt, but that I was sure the other captains, if he mentioned the subject to them, would at once inform him, that their real debts were not shown; *I* had charged the stable-jackets, which perhaps they had not done. His Lordship said, 'Your troop is the worst in the regiment; it must be your bad management.' I replied, that there had been no neglect on my part, but that it was impossible to keep my troop out of debt. His Lordship asked me the reason; I said, that the number of flannels, shirts, boots, and shoes, which had been issued to the men with a view of going on foreign service, might be one reason, but that the chief cause was the number of stable-jackets and cloth overalls which had been issued out, particularly during the last month; that I had been charged twelve pounds in the month's abstract for these articles alone, and that I had at the same time advanced the tailor twenty-two pounds from my private purse, as the greater part of the men being under stoppages, there was no fund from which to pay him. His Lordship said this reason was not sufficient, and that a less number had been issued in his time than at any former period. I withdrew. The next day, on the 8th of November, the regiment was inspected in the field by Major-General Sir Thomas Arbuthnot. He afterwards saw the rooms and the dinners, with all of which he expressed himself satisfied. After this the captains were ordered, by seniority, to have their books inspected. I received this direction from the adjutant; why it was not acted upon I do not know. I take the liberty of requesting the particular attention of the Court to the relation of the following conversation which *then* took place, as from what I stated in reply to a question put to me by the major-general, he at first drew a wrong inference as to what I had meant to imply, and of which impression in the mind of the major-general his Lordship eagerly and perseveringly availed himself, to endeavour to show, that I had come forward with complaints; but it will be seen that the cause of my troop being in debt could not have been explained, unless I had made the statement which appeared to cause his Lordship so much displeasure. I have stated that the captains were called into the office. I took that opportunity, in consequence of what Lord Brudenell had said to me the day preceding, of endeavouring to remove from the mind of the major-general any unfavourable impression which he might form, as to the state of my troop, from observing that the debt was so large, twenty-eight pounds. I therefore said, 'General, perhaps Lord Brudenell has spoken to you on the subject of my troop-debt.' The major-general replied, 'Captain Wathen, I am surprised at your surmising any thing of the sort: Lord Brudenell has not spoken to me; but I now desire an explanation.' I replied, that his Lordship had told me on the preceding day that I should have to account to him for it. The major-general upon this referred to Lord Brudenell, who hesitated; upon which the major-general said, 'O, if this is the case, Captain Wathen is perfectly right. I consider he is right, at all events, in making the circumstance known to me.' Lord Brudenell bowed in token of acquiescence, and it was intimated to me to proceed. I stated that my troop being already under stoppages, the debt had been incurred in a manner I could not prevent, by a number of new stable-jackets and cloth overalls hav-

Captain Wathen's defence.

Captain Wathen's defence.

ing been issued out, particularly during the last month, (October,) when I had been charged by the quarter-master twelve pounds for those articles, besides *several more* which had been *ordered;* that I had also been under the necessity of advancing twenty-two pounds to the tailor, as the men being already under stoppages, there was no fund from which to pay him. The major-general asked me, if this issue, of which I spoke, was an unusual one. I replied, that since I had been captain of a troop, which was now upwards of seven years, that I was not aware of there ever having been so large a proportion issued; that in regard to the stable-jackets, the colonel's clothing had, in former years, generally sufficed, with the exception of two or three jackets in the course of a twelvemonth, and that a much greater number of cloth overalls had been issued than I had ever known to be the case. The major-general rejoined, 'Pray, Captain Wathen, have you heard any thing said about this?' 'Yes, Sir.' 'What, have there been complaints about this? Did the men come to you to complain?' '*No, Sir, they did not.*' 'How have you heard *it* then?' I supposed by this question that the major-general wished to ask me how I had heard what I had just told him, about there having been, *comparatively speaking,* so many jackets and cloth overalls issued. I therefore replied, 'From my serjeant, my serjeant-major.' I added, that I had already mentioned this circumstance to his Lordship. Lord Brudenell said, '*It's false;* he never mentioned a word to me about it.' The major-general observed, 'Now Lord Brudenell, pray do restrain yourself;' and motioned with his hand to his Lordship to be silent. The major-general asked me, if those jackets had been ordered by the lieutenant-colonel without his having spoken to me about them? I said, his Lordship had not spoken to me upon the subject. Lord Brudenell, appealing to the major-general, said, 'It's not true, Sir, he knew it perfectly well.' Lord Brudenell continued, 'there have been less jackets in my time, than on any former period. I'll call the quarter-master; this captain talks about the custom of the regiment, the quarter-master will tell you.' I replied, I had stated nothing that could not be seen from an examination of my ledgers. Lord Brudenell rejoined, 'this officer is making complaints against me; now, sir,' addressing himself to the major-general, 'you allow him to go on in the same way you did the men in the field in the morning; this is the most gross *case* of MUTINY I ever knew.' Sir Thomas Arbuthnot here again said he must request Lord Brudenell to controul himself. He asked me if I had not said the men had complained. Lord Brudenell interposed, saying, 'To be sure he did, and he now wants to deny it.' I rejoined and said, I had not said what the major-general supposed. The major-general stated that he had inferred it from what I had said. Being permitted by Sir Thomas Arbuthnot to continue my explanation, I stated that I had not preferred a complaint, or even said that complaints had been made to me; that he, the major-general, had *himself* asked *me* the question if the men had complained to me, and that he would remember I had distinctly stated, '*No, sir, they have not.*' I entreated the major-general to remember my words. The major-general then admitted that *he did remember this.* I went on to observe, that in what I *had* said, I had merely wished to explain the cause of my debt, and to exculpate myself from blame in consequence of its being over the regulation; that what I said, was only in self-defence, and in my own justification. I begged *now,* however, to call the attention of the major-general to the

Captain Wathen's defence.

Captain Wathen's defence.

manner in which his Lordship had addressed me; I regretted to be obliged to state, that since I had been released from arrest, and ordered to return to my duty, I had been daily subjected to his Lordship's censure, both in the field and in quarters; that the lieutenant-colonel was perpetually telling me that it was my bad management which caused my troop to be in such a state; that it was not only the worst troop in the regiment, but in the service. Lord Brudenell observed, 'Well, sir, and is it not so?' I appealed to the major-general if this state of things could go on. I said that I had exerted myself to the utmost; that I trusted that the major-general would not find that my troop was out of order, or that I had been negligent in *any particular;* that it was most painful to me to be so spoken of; that I had never previously been so thought of by my former commanding officers. Lord Brudenell shortly after closed the discussion, by observing, 'General, the parade is now formed.' Sir Thomas Arbuthnot then dismissed me, saying, 'Sir, I shall see you again.' When the parade was finished, which lasted about twenty minutes, the captains of troops were ordered into the office, and the quarter-master. The major-general said a few words to the effect that he had been entirely satisfied with every thing he had seen; and that all would have been satisfactory, if it had not been for a complaint put forward by Captain Wathen relative to the men being dissatisfied about the issue of clothing. The major-general went on to ask if the stable-jackets furnished was an unusual issue, to which I bowed and assented; he continuing, asked if the men had expressed discontent, to which a negative was given; and *I* then said, 'Excuse me, general, I made no such complaint.' 'Well, but you said you had heard it from your serjeant.' 'Sir, you have misunderstood me;

I did not refer to discontent, I said I had heard it from my serjeant—my serjeant-major, he is clerk to me, and it was natural he should point out the reason of my debt being so heavy.' 'Well, but surely, Captain Wathen, you said the men complained.' 'Excuse me, sir, I did not say so.' 'But you said they grumbled then.' 'No, sir, I do not permit them to grumble to me.' 'Well, my aide-de-camp was present, and your Lordship's adjutant, if he was not too much occupied with his papers to listen.' Captain Corkran then remarked, 'I *inferred*, from what Captain Wathen had said, that he had heard through the serjeant that the men had complained.' I replied, that Captain Corkran had misunderstood me. I then added, if he reflected, he would recollect that it was not *I* who had said the men complained, but the major-general who asked *me* if they *did;* and the major-general will no doubt recollect that I immediately replied, '*No, sir, they have not.*' The major-general again intimated that he did recollect this. During the second interview I wished to call the major-general's attention to Lord Brudenell's conduct to me; but Sir Thomas Arbuthnot interrupted me, and said, 'THAT I cannot now attend to, as I am here only on matters of finance:' and we were then shortly dismissed.

Captain Wathen's defence.

"In relating to the Court the conversation which took place in the regimental office, in the presence of the major-general, in regard to the debt of my troop, I have omitted to mention an occurrence which took place. When I stated that my men were already under stoppages, Lord Brudenell observed to the major-general that this was not the case—that some days ago, on looking at my weekly mess-book, which showed the numbers of men under stoppages, he had been surprised to see how few they were, and had in consequence sent for my serjeant

Captain Wathen's defence.

major, to ask him why there were not *more men* under stoppages.' Lord Brudenell continued, 'If you will allow me, general, I will send for this book.' The book was accordingly sent for, but on its being produced, Lord Brudenell looked at it, *put it aside*, and did *not show* it to the major-general. I now produce it to the Court, and it will be seen that the greater part of the men, more than half of them, were, at the time alluded to, and as I had stated, under stoppages to the amount of sixpence per diem of their pay. On the evening of the day in question, the 8th of November, on which the major-general had inspected the regiment in the field, the adjutant told me, that there was no written order; but that captains and officers commanding troops were to make known to their men what the major-general had said about the conduct and appearance of the regiment. I said 'Very well,' and went to evening stables for that purpose. Before going into any stables my troop-serjeant met me; I told him I had come to evening stables for the purpose of stating to the men what the major-general had said in praise of the regiment. He replied, 'The orderly officer has already read the order.' I rejoined, that I was not aware that there had been a written order given out; but that I would, notwithstanding, state in each stable what I had been directed to say. This I did, not because I thought it necessary—the order in question having been already read by the orderly officer—but from the conviction I had been compelled to entertain, that the lieutenant-colonel would be likely to avail himself, to my disadvantage, of any circumstance that might by possibility be construed into a dereliction of duty. The major-general, upon a subsequent day, Monday, the 11th of November, resumed his inspection of the regiment. Previously to looking at the men's kitts he sent for me, and *again* referred to the impressions he had formed; that I had stated that there had been complaints about the issue of clothing, and desired me to send for the serjeant who had informed me. I reminded the major-general of my having REPEATEDLY DISAVOWED having said what he supposed; and that he would remember I had done so, on *the instant* that he had made known to me that he had drawn such an inference from what I had said. The major-general replied, 'Well, I *inferred* from what you said, that you had stated your men complained; you know I *pressed you very hard* upon the subject, and I must say that you contradicted me in a very flat manner, though I am quite willing to believe you did not mean me offence, and were probably not aware of it yourself.' I said I felt obliged to him for excusing me, and earnestly requested the major-general to pardon me, if, under the trying circumstances of the case, I had said any thing which caused him displeasure. The major-general appeared satisfied; and I fell in with my troop. Upon his making an inspection of my kitts, which were placed upon the ground in front of the men, the lieutenant-colonel called for a stable-jacket belonging to private William Hopkins, which he showed to the major-general, saying, 'This fellow came to me to complain of a new stable-jacket being ordered for him, and he seemed to consider that it was a violent grievance that I should order him a new one. Now look at it,' showing the old one. The major-general said that he considered as the pay of the cavalry soldier was so good, that the man ought to have a new jacket. Upon which Lord Brudenell flung the jacket at the man, saying, 'There, sir;' then turning to me, his Lordship continued, 'I can tell you, sir, you shall have plenty more new jackets in your troop."

Captain Wathen's defence.

Captain Wathen's defence.

" I shall now relate the circumstance named in the sixth Charge, which caused my arrest. On the 12th of November, after the mess dinner, between one and two o'clock P. M. the adjutant came to me in the mess-room, and said the colonel wanted me in the office. I went there immediately. There was no one present but the lieutenant-colonel and the adjutant. Lord Brudenell said to me, ' Captain Wathen, did you read the orders to the men on Friday evening, when the major-general dined at the mess after the inspection, or rather did you state to them what officers commanding troops had been verbally desired by me to state ?' I said I had. ' Was this before or after the orderly officer went round ?' ' I do not at this moment recollect.' ' What did you say to them ?' I must here observe that I now perceived that the adjutant was again taking down in writing what I said. I replied to Lord Brudenell's question, that I said to the men, that I had received the colonel's instructions to convey to them the entire approbation their appearance and steadiness in the field had called forth from the major-general, as well as their excellent conduct in quarters since the regiment had been under the major-general's command. ' Did you say any thing more to them ?' ' I do not think I did, nothing that I can recollect.' ' Did you address them on the Saturday night ?' ' No, I did not.' ' On Sunday night ?' ' No.' ' Did you addres them last night ?' ' I read the orders to them, according to your Lordship's instructions.' ' Did you say any thing else to them ?' ' No : I did not, my Lord.' ' It's very extraordinary ; you may go, sir, and I'll send for you again.' I retired, and went immediately to my own room. In about a quarter of an hour I was sent for again to the office, and again his Lordship cross-examined me at some length upon what I had previously stated. When his Lordship appeared to have finished questioning me, I then said, 'Pray, my Lord, may I inquire on what account these questions are put to me?' His Lordship said, 'Yes, I'll tell you. It has been reported to me, from three different sources in the regiment, that on Saturday night you assembled your men, that you addressed them, that you told them you were very much pleased with them, that the left troop of the line had been particularly admired, that you made some allusion about going on service, and had said your heart was with them.' I replied, 'My Lord, I see now what is meant; your informant is wrong in some respects, and has not expressed the words I made use of. It was not on Saturday night, as you have been informed, that I spoke to my men, but on Saturday, after mid-day stables. And I shall now voluntarily inform your Lordship what passed.' I then recapitulated, as nearly as possible, the whole substance of what I afterwards committed to writing in the letter which his Lordship laid before the Court.

Captain Wathen's defence.

"Having stated this, his Lordship proceeded to cross-examine very closely, and I answered all the interrogatories put to me, although his Lordship frequently endeavoured to make me contradict my statement; at these times I reminded his Lordship that I had already stated the contrary. The lieutenant-colonel turned to the adjutant, and said, 'Have you got all that down, Mr. Hecker?' The adjutant replied, 'No; I cannot follow Captain Wathen, he speaks too fast for me to follow him in writing.' Lord Brudenell said, 'Now, then, you'll state over again all that passed?' I replied, 'As my words are to be taken down, had I not better give it to your Lordship in writing?' His Lordship said, 'I am not to be dictated to, the way I am to command *my* regiment; I choose to have it verbally, and you'll state it all over again.' I said, 'My Lord, the adjutant, it appears, has already taken my statement at length, together with my replies to your Lordship's cross-examination; I am perfectly ready to give it you in writing also.' His Lordship said, 'I shall do nothing of the sort.' He commanded me immediately to state over again (for the adjutant to take down) what I had said to my men. I replied, that situated as I found myself, I must decline saying any more, that I would give it him in writing.—'This is disobedience of orders; you positively refuse to obey my commands, do you?' 'My Lord, I decline saying any more.' 'But *you shall.* I now *order you, I command you.*' I was silent. 'Now, Sir, do you disobey my *commands?* I here most solemnly declare, that as I am commanding officer of this regiment, if you don't comply with my orders, you shall be placed under arrest.' His Lordship appeared extraordinarily excited, his countenance was changed, and he made great gesticulations. I said, I was willing to state to his Lordship, in writing, what had passed. He then said, 'You shall do it in this office: *come here, Sir, you sha'n't go away;* now sit down here, and write it.' I replied, 'My Lord, under present circumstances I might well require consideration, but since you so command me, I have no objection to sit down here at once and write what passed.'

"I sat down and commenced writing immediately, and had written two pages and a half when his Lordship came to me and said, 'Captain Wathen, you must be writing a great deal more than what you said to your men; you can't require so much time for that; give me what you have written.' I replied, 'My Lord, I am in the middle of my letter, you shall have it the moment it is finished.' He said, 'It is time for parade, give it to me;' and his Lordship approached me, apparently with the view of receiving my paper. I withheld it from him, and said, 'Excuse me, my Lord, I cannot give you an unfinished letter.' He rejoined, 'Then you can finish it after parade.' I answered, 'Very well, Sir,' and putting it in my pocket, was withdrawing, when his Lordship replied, 'You shall not take it out of the office; give it to me, Sir! Do you dare to disobey my commands?' I said, 'My Lord, I cannot give up an unfinished document.' 'Then put it in that box till you come back from parade, *I* sha'n't read it; *the adjutant* will be upon parade with you, *all* the officers will be there together, you will all leave parade together, so you can have no objection.' 'My Lord, I decline leaving my letter.' 'Then, sir, you disobey my positive commands—Mr. Hecker, bring in some witnesses.' The adjutant shortly returned from parade with the two senior officers that were there—Captain Wood and Lieutenant Wakefield.

Captain Wathen's defence.

"The Court are already aware of the circumstances which then took place, which were followed by my being placed in arrest. The first step I took on leaving the office was to copy and finish the letter alluded to, and enclose it to his Lordship, with the following one.

"*Cork Barracks, November* 12, 1833,
Quarter past 4, P. M.

"MY LORD,

"I have now the honour to enclose the copy of the letter which I wrote in your office about half-past two P. M. and in a finished state. The original document I retain, which your Lordship can refer to at any time, should you wish to do so.

"I have the honour, &c. &c.
(Signed) "A. WATHEN,
"Captain 15th King's Hussars.

"*To Lieutenant-Colonel Lord Brudenell,*
Commanding King's Hussars."

Captain Wathen's defence.

"I cannot of course be positive as to the exact words I made use of in speaking to the men; I did not reflect on the matter before-hand, and should certainly never have thought of the circumstance again, had not his Lordship obliged me to do so by attaching so much importance to the occurrence. I can only be certain, that the import and substance of what I said is put down, and is correct; and I cannot but think that my having so spoken to the men had a very good effect, and that it was afterwards evinced upon the occasion of the major-general concluding his inspection, as he was pleased to bestow the highest encomiums upon every thing he saw, and he remarked upon the manner in which the bits and irons in my troop in particular were cleaned, and the order in the stables.

"I feel that I may have perhaps trespassed upon the patience of the Court in making the narration which I have concluded, but I trust it will be found that I have not entered into any matter that was irrelevant to the subject, and as it is the object of my present judges to elicit the truth, and to ascertain the real circumstances of the case, I feel certain they are not the less disposed to grant the subject their unwearied attention, and that I shall only be meeting their wishes in calling upon them to devote such portion of their valuable time to the consideration of what I have further to relate, as the circumstances of the case may require.

"From what I have already stated, and from the evidence which has been elicited from the cross-examination of the witnesses for the prosecution, the Court will now be aware of the position in which I was placed with regard to the lieutenant-colonel, and the judgment which I might have been justified in forming, as to his intentions in demanding of me to deliver up to him, or into his possession, my unfinished letter. I have now arrived at that period of my defence, where I can with advantage to myself examine the just value which should be attached to the charges preferred against me; and I trust, that the Court, having taken into consideration the statements I have made, and which I consider to have been already in a great degree borne out, will have no difficulty in following me in the conclusions which I shall wish to deduce. Captain Wathen's defence.

"In considering the six charges preferred against me, the Court will doubtless perceive that four out of the number, viz. the first, second, third, and fifth charges, are principally endeavoured to be supported upon the recollections of others as to what I may, or may not have said, or intended to express, in conversations and discussions which have passed away. Whatever in these charges is tangible and ostensible, I am ready to meet and can disprove; such, for instance, (and which I humbly conceive to be an essential point,) as to whether or not the stable-jackets and cloth overalls issued and charged to the men of my troop was or was not an *unusual issue*, and whether such issue *was* or *was* not, the principal cause of the debt of my troop exceeding the regulation. But those parts which merely depend upon the memory of others, and the impressions they may have formed on discussions which took place in the orderly room, but do not tax me with specific *acts* or *neglects*, are of a more vague nature, and although perhaps the least important, the Court will perceive that the proceedings are more than doubled by the necessity entailed upon me of disproving those parts of the charges. Words spoken, conversations and discussions which have passed away, are difficult to be recalled and presented in their true colours, to those who were not present when they took place. This, of course, is an obstacle which must effect the prosecutor equally with the defendant; but if it were the wish or intention on the part of the former, to make up charges, (if I may be permitted the expression,) and grounds were wanting, this course would naturally present itself, as being the best calculated for such a purpose; as although a charge founded on circumstances of this nature may be difficult to prove, it is also less easy to be met on the part of the defendant, in a direct and obvious manner. Another circumstance, which it would have been desirable to have avoided, is the necessity that this part of the prosecution has induced of calling upon the major-general commanding the district, as a witness.

"I have, in consequence of this circumstance, been obliged to detail at length, and comment upon the conversations and discussions of a general officer, which I could very much wish to have avoided, and which nothing but the urgency of the circumstances would have prevailed upon me to do. I may here remark, that I trust it will appear quite evident to this honourable Court, that the three first charges must have been framed at the instigation of the lieutenant-colonel, and never would have been brought against me, but for the conversation and events of Tuesday the 12th of November. The offences which these three charges exhibit against me were said to be committed on Friday the 8th of November, and notwithstanding the seriousness of the crimes, I was permitted to continue to do duty till his Lordship prevailed upon the major-general to think that I had not cleared up the misconception he laboured under, or made sufficient atonement for the contradiction that misapprehension of my words led to; will it be believed that the major-general, if such was his own unbiassed opinion, would have allowed me to do duty, or remain at large an hour? besides which, the major-general has stated to this Court, that he took no part in framing any of the five last charges, and I am sure the Court must believe him, though the lieutenant-colonel has affirmed that all the charges were submitted to him, and that he consulted with him upon them. Captain Wathen's defence.

" The following observations which were made with regard to the trials of Captain John Cameron and Captain and Adjutant John Ray, in 1799, will not, I think, be inapposite.

" 'His Majesty, adverting to what has in some measure appeared in the course of both these trials, has expressed his extreme disapprobation of keeping charges against an officer or soldier in reserve, until they shall have accumulated, and then bringing them before a general Court-Martial collectively ; whereas every charge should be preferred at the time the fact or facts on which it turns are recent, or if knowingly passed over, ought not, either in candour or in justice, to be in future brought into question.'

" I will now proceed to the consideration of the first charge.

First Charge.

" ' For that he, Captain Wathen, of the 15th Hussars, did on the 8th of November, 1833, at Cork, at the half-yearly inspection of the 15th Hussars, voluntarily state, in an invidious and improper manner to Major-General Sir Thomas Arbuthnot, than an unusual supply of stable-jackets had been issued to the men of his troop, and which had been sent from the tailor's shop without his knowledge, thereby imputing improper conduct to Lieutenant-Colonel Lord Brudenell, his commanding officer, although it is the custom of the service to issue new stable-jackets to cavalry soldiers as they may require them.'

Captain Wathen's defence.

" The first accusation in this charge is the having made a voluntary statement. It has been proved by the direct evidence of Lieutenant and Adjutant Hecker, that on the day previous to the inspection, I had been blamed by the lieutenant-colonel on account of my troop debt, and that an invidious comparison between my troop and others had been drawn by the lieutenant-colonel. Lord Brudenell and Captain Corkran have shown that I mentioned to the major-general at the inspection, that I thought it necessary to explain the cause of my troop debt, in consequence of Lord Brudenell having told me on a previous day that I must acount to the major-general for the circumstance: and I shall hereafter call upon Major Sir Walter Scott, and Captain Rose, as corroborative evidence, that his Lordship did so forewarn me. Had I neglected to do so, it will be seen that a false impression would have been left upon the mind of the major-general in consequence of the unfounded remarks in regard to the debt of my troop inserted in the regimental return. Might not my silence upon the subject have been considered a tacit acknowledgment that I wished to avoid inquiry about the debt, and should I not have left myself in the power of the lieutenant-colonel to demand of me before the general, why I had not explained the cause, as he had told me I should be obliged to do, particularly as I observed Captain Corkran, aide-de-camp, examining the paper which showed the amount of it. Captains are held responsible by his Majesty's regulations, that the accounts of their troops and companies are properly kept; and, under the circumstances in which I was placed, I feel confident that there is not a member of this Court who does not acquit me of any impropriety in having explained to the general officer who examined my accounts, the cause of the excess of the troop debt. As to its being voluntary, or not, I can only say, that had I not considered myself compelled to do so in consequence of the forewarning of Lord Brudenell, as well as in self-defence, I should not most certainly have mentioned the circumstance. The next point to be examined is, as to my statement having been made in an invidious and improper manner to the major-general.

Captain Wathen's defence.

" In considering this part of the charge, it is but justice to me that the position in which I was placed, with regard to the major-general, and the lieutenant-colonel, should be borne in mind.

" The lieutenant-colonel was upon intimate and friendly terms with the major-general; on my part, I could not boast the honour of his personal acquaintance; but had it been permitted to refer to former transactions, I could have shown that representations of a very injurious tendency in regard to my conduct had been made by the lieutenant-colonel, and which must still have remained on the mind of the major-general, as I never had any means of personal intercourse, or by letter, any opportunity of answering them. It will, therefore, be apparent to the Court, that I was very disadvantageously situated; and when, in addition to the circumstances I have mentioned, it is observed, that at the time I made the explanation in regard to the cause of the debt of my troop, the lieutenant-colonel endeavoured to impress the major-general with the idea that I was making a complaint, (as has been shown by the evidence of Lieutenant and Adjutant Hecker,) it will not appear surprising that Major-General Sir Thomas Arbuthnot, influenced by previous impressions, should have viewed my conduct in a more unfavourable light than he would have done had he been in possession of the information which is now before the Court.

Captain Wathen's defence.

"I have now replied to the charge of my statement having been voluntary, invidious, and improper; but the manner of my making such a statement is not the total of the charge—that I *did* make a statement AT ALL, and therein say, 'that an unusual supply of stable-jackets had been issued to the men of my troop,' is also a part of it. The having made a statement upon this subject, I have no cause, and it is not my wish to disavow; it is only necessary that I should show that it was correct. In order to do so, I refer to the quarter-master's returns upon the table, which have already been examined, and to the troop returns which I now produce. By these returns it will appear, that in regard to stable-jackets, more have been issued within the last three months than in the sum total of the nine preceding years added together. With respect to cloth overalls, the Court will observe that no mention is made of this article of clothing in the charge, but it will be found from the evidence given by the major-general, that at the time *I* mentioned the subject, I stated to him that an unusual supply of stable-jackets and *cloth overalls*, combining the two, was the principal cause of the debt of my troop. On reference to the returns, and any of the troop ledgers from which they have been made up, it is shown that there has been a *general* issue of cloth overalls at *one* period, every effective man being supplied with a pair in the month of March last, at his own expense, and some of them with *two pairs*, and also a new jacket within the year. Having been censured by the lieutenant-colonel on account of my troop being in debt, and told it was more than that of any other, and that I should have to account for the circumstance to the major-general, I felt myself justified in bringing under his notice what I have now represented to the Court; indeed not only justified, but called

Captain Wathen's defence.

upon to do so. In fact, I did not consider myself safe in withholding an explanation. In representing the circumstance I made as little allusion as I possibly could to any other troop in the regiment, much less (as is proved by the major-general's evidence) to the custom or usages in this respect, of any other regiment. The lieutenant-colonel has, however, deemed it necessary to summon the lieutenant colonel commanding the 7th Dragoon Guards, and the quarmaster, Mr. Johnson, on the occasion. The cloth worn by the two regiments being different in colour, the criterion would not have been just. Scarlet cloth might, perhaps, be equally durable, if not more so, than blue; but it would certainly be more liable to receive stains, and would therefore, as a fatigue dress, be oftener replaced by new. The remaining part of the charge consists in the alleged accusation, of my having stated to the major-general that the stable-jackets had been sent from the tailor's shop without my knowledge, thereby imputing improper conduct to Lord Brudenell. In reply to this, I can only state, that I am not aware of having ever mentioned a word about the tailor's shop; but if I had done so, I should have been perfectly justified, as I do not even know where it is; but it is not my intention to occupy the valuable time of the Court by quibbling upon words; under other circumstances, and had I felt a difficulty in establishing a defence, I might, perhaps, have been justified in dwelling more at length upon such points. In that case, and had I been so disposed, the present charges would have afforded me ample opportunity of commenting upon and pointing out discrepancies. The part of the charge alluded to, is probably founded upon the answer being given by me to the major-general, when asked by him if the order had been given without my knowledge. I replied that it had. It remained

Captain Wathen's defence.

for his Lordship to have proved to the contrary, which would have been impossible, as he never did make known to me, or consult with me in regard to the ordering of the new jackets and cloth overalls in question. As to the inference drawn by his Lordship in the charge, that I imputed to him improper conduct, I can only say that such was not my intention. I was bound in duty and in self-defence to state what I did, according to his forewarning. I said nothing but undisguised truth, and if in so doing, his Lordship's conduct appeared in a disadvantageous point of view, the fault did not rest with me, neither do I feel myself called upon to answer the inferences which may have been deduced by his Lordship. With regard to the last sentence, that it is the custom of the service to issue new stable-jackets to cavalry soldiers as they may require them, I never dissented from this view of the subject, and have nothing whatever to object to the observation. The major-general has shown that I merely designated the issue as *unusual*, and that only in reference to the regiment I belong to.

Second Charge.

" 'For conduct unbecoming the character of an officer and a gentleman, in first having stated to Major-General Sir Thomas Arbuthnot, on Friday, the said 8th of November, at the place aforesaid, 'that he had been informed by the serjeants of his troop, that the men were discontented at having new stable-jackets delivered out to them.' Such a statement being contrary to the fact; and having afterwards, on the same day, in an improper and disrespectful manner, when addressed by the major-general, denied having made the above statement; which denial, he, Captain Wathen, repeated to the major-general on the Monday following.'

"The first point to which it will be necessary to draw the attention of the Court, is the allegation in the second charge, that I stated to the major-general *that I had been informed* by the *serjeants* of my troop, that the men were discontented at having new stable-jackets issued out to them. This charge is only supported upon the recollection of others, as to a conversation which had passed away, and which took place at a moment when all parties may naturally be supposed to have been excited, and, consequently liable to misconceive, or put a wrong construction upon what was said. I must also entreat the Court to keep in sight the disadvantageous position in which I was placed, with regard to the officers present on the occasion, and that the major-general and his aide-de-camp might, from previous circumstances, have been disposed to think that I was a person likely to complain; under this impression they would have been more readily liable to misinterpret my words, and to attach such meaning to them, as it has been shown by Lieutenant and Adjutant Hecker, was pointed out by Lieutenant-Colonel Lord Brudenell, in opposition to my explanation. The major-general has stated, 'When I asked Captain Wathen if the men had made complaints to him, he replied, they had not!' The charge itself does not accuse me of having stated that I had heard complaints from my men, but that I had been informed by my serjeants that discontent existed. What gave rise to the supposition, that I meant to express that the men were discontented, is easily explained. With reference to what was passing in conversation, the major-general put a question to me, as to how I had heard *it;* my reply was, I had heard IT from my serjeant, my serjeant-major, and upon *this* monosyllable has hinged the misconception. I supposed the general alluded, in this

Captain Wathen's defence.

Captain Wathen's defence.

question, to what *I* had just before mentioned, and which was uppermost in my mind, namely, that there had been an unusual issue, which was the cause of my debt, and the major-general, being probably more occupied with the idea of ascertaining if there were dissatisfactions, or complaints, alluded to that circumstance, and applied my answer accordingly. What possible motive could I have had, in making a statement to the major-general, that my men had been dissatisfied, and complained to the serjeant, when so shortly afterwards I took every means to remove that impression from the mind of the major-general? If my men had complained to the serjeant, it would have been my duty, first to investigate the cause before I reported it to the commanding officer; and not having done so, I should be arming the lieutenant-colonel with power to find fault for so serious an omission—an act of folly, it is very unlikely any person, much less one placed in the critical situation I was with my commanding-officer, would be guilty of. It was then *time present*, and if I had had an intention to complain, or wilfully misrepresent, I should not have withdrawn my words. I could have had no object in so doing; but surely it is unfair that a man should be held responsible for the constructions that others (in consequence of previous impressions formed) may have been induced to put upon his words. I, at the time of the conversation taking place, explained my meaning, and stated what it was I wished to express. I could do no more than this, on perceiving that my words had been misunderstood. The witnesses against me, including the prosecutor, have requested to be permitted to correct their sworn testimony, deliberately given, after upwards of six or seven weeks' consideration; and no objection was offered, either on my part or on that of the Court. I shall point to one instance, which appears to be peculiarly apposite. In the cross-examination of Lieutenant-Colonel Lord Brudenell, upon the sixth charge, the substance of a question from the Court to his Lordship, is as follows: 'How do you reconcile your statement with what you have alleged in the fifth charge?' and his Lordship replies to the effect, 'That he had not stated what the Court supposed, that his answer (which created the misconception) referred to another circumstance!'

Captain Wathen's defence.

"On my part, and with reference to the conversation in the regimental office, on the 8th of November, I have shown that I gave a similar explanation. The major-general had alluded to one circumstance, and I, in my answer, to another; and I trust that this honourable Court will not refuse me the indulgence, in this respect, which it has granted to the prosecutor and the witnesses for the prosecution, and that I shall consequently be exonerated upon this part of the charge.

"The lieutenant-colonel and non-commissioned officers have clearly shown that discontent existed amongst the men, and also that the major-general was aware of it; but if *I* did not set it forth, the sentence in the charge, 'such statement being contrary to fact,' does not affect me. I believe it to be the present understanding of the Court, from what has been stated in the prosecution, that the demur made by hussar Hopkins was, to the expense of repairing his jacket; whereas it was not so, but to being furnished with a new one, when the old one was repairable; and here I think I may ask, what inducement I could have had to make an untrue statement, when, if my motives had been vindictive or vicious, I had the power to prove the men were dissatisfied; but I did no such thing, it was my anxious wish and intention to show my troop to the

Captain Wathen's defence.

major-general in the most advantageous point of view, as I have every reason to believe the lieutenant-colonel would endeavour to impress upon his mind, that it was, what he described it, the worst in the regiment. This, I am sure, will be admitted as undeniable proof how much my words and meaning have been misconceived. Another part of the charge against me is, that 'I denied having made the assertion imputed to me.' I at once admit the fact; it has been shown in evidence that I *did* deny having made the assertion; not only at the moment I discovered the misconstruction which had been put upon my meaning by the major-general, but upon every subsequent occasion on which it was alluded to. So far from any attempt to disprove having done so, I press the fact upon the notice of the Court; I feel persuaded that in their opinion this circumstance will exculpate me. The remaining part of the charge relates to the denial alluded to having been made to the major-general in an improper and disrespectful manner. The lieutenant-colonel appears to be particularly alive to my conduct towards the major-general. In the preceding, as well as in the present charge, it will be observed, that disrespect to the major-general, not to Lord Brudenell, is preferred against me. It appears extraordinary, that his Lordship should thus usurp the privilege of the major-general, and stand forward to defend that officer, as if he were unable to judge for himself, and to take his own measures with regard to those under his command.

"The major-general has stated that I contradicted him upon the occasion of his having stated I had said the men complained; but he has also qualified this by saying, he had expressed a hope and willingness to believe I had not meant to offend him; and I must add, that after such an admission, it does appear strange to me, that the major-general should have lent himself to assist in framing a charge upon the circumstance, without making known to me his intentions. My conduct, in denying the assertion, is termed by the prosecutor improper and disrespectful. I entreat the Court to consider the circumstances under which I was placed, in making such denial. I perceived that the prosecutor, with unremitting perseverance, was endeavouring to establish in the mind of the major-general an erroneous impression, to be made use of to my disadvantage. I gave explanations; but they did not appear to be attended to, and I found that nothing but the most positive disavowal on my part could set my conduct in its true light; and if I had not done so, the Court will now perceive, whether or not I should, at the present moment, have been in a position effectually to disprove three out of the six charges, which are now preferred against me. I regret that my manner or mode of expression should at any time have been impolite; and I confess that I was hurt and irritated, not only at Lord Brudenell's language, (which has been termed so *simply* an *objectionable* expression,) but at the anxiety demonstrated, to induce me to assent to having made use of words which I never uttered, and which I had, as shown by the evidence of the major-general, repeatedly disavowed.

Captain Wathen's defence.

"I have but one more remark to offer upon this charge, and to which I have already alluded; namely, that I am not charged with having evinced impropriety and disrespect towards the prosecutor himself; and such being the case, it may be necessary, previously to coming to a decision upon my conduct, to consider how far the lieutenant-colonel is authorized in accusing me, as it. were, on the part of the major-general commanding the district, when that officer must appear to have settled all matters

Captain Wathen's defence.

connected with the subject of the charges, at the time he questioned me in relation to it on the Monday afternoon, when it must be supposed he accepted my apology, as he gave me no reason to think otherwise; and his aide-de-camp has stated that he appeared to be perfectly satisfied. Lord Brudenell never said one word to me on the subject of the disrespect to the major-general, which he now prefers as a charge; and Sir Thomas Arbuthnot himself has shown, that when he pointed out to me my error, that I immediately made him every apology in my power; I may fairly ask, if it would be possible for me to suppose, under these circumstances, that what had taken place *then*, would be again referred to, and made the subject for a charge?

Third Charge.

" 'For conduct unbecoming the character of an officer and a gentleman, in stating to Major-General Sir Thomas Arbuthnot, on the said 8th of November, at the place aforesaid, that 'he had reported or mentioned to Lieutenant-colonel Lord Brudenell, that the men of his troop had expressed discontent at having new stable-jackets delivered out to them, which statement was directly contrary to truth and fact.'

" The defence upon this third charge appears to be so entirely comprised in that of the preceding one, that if I have succeeded in vindicating my conduct in regard to the accusation contained in it, viz. the second charge, this also must appear to have been already replied to and disproved. I shall, therefore, have but few remarks to offer regarding it: it must be apparent that the present charge, as well as part of the preceding, is founded upon the misconception which may, at one moment, have existed upon the mind of

Captain Wathen's defence.

the major-general as to what I had said, or intended to say, at an early period of the discussion in question. The witnesses for the prosecution are the only evidence; and unfortunately for me, my defence may, in some measure, be considered to depend upon their memories and inferences; and here I think I may be pardoned for remarking upon the many misconceptions and mistakes made by those officers during the course of their examinations upon this trial; and it will therefore be apparent to the Court, that at the time of the conversation alluded to in the regimental office taking place, they may equally have been subject to form erroneous impressions, and to misconceive my meaning.

"If I have succeeded in showing that there was a misconception, and that when I said I had heard IT, I must have alluded to what was the cause of the debt, and not to complaints having been made, it will by a parity of reasoning be seen, that this charge being founded upon the same conversation and assertion, I am equally to be acquitted.

"Captain Corkran has stated, in answer to a question from the prosecutor, that he believes I said I had heard IT from my serjeant; and he adds, he thinks I said I had reported IT to my colonel. It will be obvious, that what I alluded to in the one case, I did in the other; and I shall therefore not detain the Court by a recapitulation of arguments which I feel to be unnecessary.

"I fully believe the Court will acquit me upon the three charges I have now gone into, and I regret to be compelled any longer to detain the Court upon the subject; but as they are so completely interwoven, I may perhaps be permitted to state those material points, which appear to me to have been adduced in my favour, in the evidence of the wit-

Captain Wathen's defence.

nesses for the prosecution, and which apply to these charges generally. It has been acknowledged that the remarks upon the debt and credit returns, in regard to all the troops except mine, were *added* solely at the suggestion of the major-general; that I took the earliest opportunity to remove from his mind the impression that I was making complaints against my commanding officer; and it is admitted, that I never stated that I had heard complaints from my men, and that it was supposed the major-general had accepted my explanation and apology, as he appeared perfectly satisfied.

"It is clearly proved that my commanding officer was neither amicable nor friendly to me; and the whole of the witnesses for the prosecution have endeavoured to explain and correct their evidence. The prosecutor himself admits that I used no very objectionable words; and that *the utmost he can recollect*, was my observation of 'I did not say so.' He further states, that the major-general did *not comment upon my conduct* at the time, as represented; and I can myself conscientiously affirm, that I have no recollection of the circumstance, neither is the assertion borne out by the evidence. It has been attempted to be shown in the prosecution, that in my troop there was a greater proportion of defaulters amongst the men, and of broken knees amongst the horses, than in any other troop. The returns I now produce to the Court will show how far this assertion has been borne out. Another accusation was then introduced, that there were at one period more horses with sore backs in my troop, than in any other. This charge would as readily have been disproved as that of the defaulters and broken-kneed horses, had it been also possible that correct returns could be produced; but as the sores no longer remain, and at the

Captain Wathen's defence.

time of their existence it depended upon the officer commanding a troop to support such cases only as he thought necessary, no just estimate can be formed. I could easily have elicited the state of the regiment in this respect, during the cross-examination, had I been actuated by any other motive than that of repelling the accusation in the charges; but I avoided doing so, not because I feared discussion, being enabled to prove, that upon an average, there did not exist a greater proportion of sore backs in my troop, than in others of the service squadrons; and the senior-major has already borne testimony that there was no want of zeal and attention on my part; but I avoided it, because I considered such matter is irrelevant and improper. The Lieutenant-colonel was particularly anxious that the subject should be concealed; and at a parade, just before the inspection, his Lordship addressed the regiment most urgently, and requested that the number of sore backs, which he informed us amounted to forty-nine, might be kept a regimental secret.

"The accusation produced against me has obliged me, in self-defence, to speak upon the subject, and has relieved me from the onus of discovering his Lordship's secret! I shall bring evidence to prove the evil was general, and not confined to any particular troop, and that upon an average they suffered alike in this respect; and that it arose from the low condition of the horses, caused by excessive hard work at Newbridge, from which they had not thoroughly recovered, on the arrival of the regiment in these quarters, when the long and rapid drills were resumed and continued. The evidence I shall produce, will elicit the real state of the case; and I shall not, therefore, unnecessarily detain the Court upon the subject, but proceed to the fourth charge.

Captain Wathen's defence.

Fourth Charge.

" 'For conduct unbecoming the character of an officer and a gentleman, in having in a letter addressed to his said commanding officer, Lieutenant-Colonel Lord Brudenell, dated 12th November 1833, made a statement contrary to truth and fact, viz., that in compliance with instructions conveyed to him by the adjutant on the evening of the said 8th of November, after the inspection, he had assembled his troop after evening stables, to convey to them the major-general's approbation of their appearance, &c., whereas he, Captain Wathen, did not on that evening obey Lieutenant-Colonel Lord Brudenell's orders to the above effect, conveyed to him through the adjutant.'

" The Court have already been made aware, and have doubtless received the information with surprise, that no complaint was made to me upon the subject of the matter contained in this fourth charge, until it was put forward against me, by the Lieutenant-colonel, in its present serious form. The first time I learnt his Lordship's dissatisfaction, or could even surmise that he considered that there had been any neglect on my part, or that blame could attach to me upon the subject, was when I received the charge against me, and the *present* is the *first* and *only* occasion on which his Lordship has called upon me to answer to such accusation, or give explanation upon any circumstance relating to it in the shape of a complaint. Had he done so, I could at once have proved to him, that I was not in fault, and have made the truth apparent to him, which would have prevented the necessity for this public investigation. If his Lordship believed that there were grounds for the charge which he now at length puts forward against me, is it not extraordinary that he did not at the time make some intimation to me upon the subject? Previously to representing my conduct to head-quarters in so odious a light, is it not to be wondered at, that, standing in the responsible situation of lieutenant-colonel commanding the regiment, his Lordship should not have felt himself compelled by his duty, as well as in honour and in justice, to call upon me for explanation, and if such had not appeared satisfactory to him, to have informed me of the steps he was about to pursue, before he made his report? Ought he not, as a primary measure, to have apprised me that circumstances had led him to suppose that I had been guilty of negligence in the non-performance of a duty, and of a still greater offence, in telling an untruth upon the subject?

Captain Wathen's defence.

"It must appear to every member of this Court, that the Lieutenant-colonel not making any such communication to me, was most unhandsome, and in opposition to the usages of the service; and his Lordship's procedure in this respect must certainly have subjected him to the suspicion that he was influenced in his conduct upon this occasion by a wish to take me by surprise, and consequently afford me less opportunity of vindicating myself upon the charge. All that ever passed between his Lordship and myself upon this subject, I have already related. It merely consisted in his Lordship's asking me if I had complied with his order, in making known to my men the praise the major-general had bestowed upon them. I replied in the affirmative, and informed him of what I had said. He further asked me if I had done so previous or subsequent to the orderly officer having gone round. I replied, (as was the case,) that I was not at that moment aware, that I did not clearly recollect. His Lordship appeared satisfied on this matter; he made no accusation, and afforded me no reason

Captain Wathen's defence.

to suppose that he doubted the truth of my replies *upon this point,* although he cross-examined me upon others, and more particularly as to what I had said to the troop upon a *subsequent occasion.* If his Lordship *did* consider that I had neglected a duty, or had told an untruth, it is evident that he must have had some particular motive in concealing his suspicions, as he said nothing to me upon the subject; and although it is now apparent that he had at the time made a complaint to the major-general with reference to it, and which was forwarded to the Horse Guards, the first intimation I received upon the subject was at the time the charge was delivered to me. It is true, a communication from the adjutant to the effect, 'That the correspondence connected with my arrest had been forwarded to Dublin,' was made known to me, but from this I could not by possibility infer, that any complaint of the nature set forth in the charge had been made against me.

"Fortunately for myself, I have had no difficulty in proving, (and I trust to the entire satisfaction of the Court,) that I neither neglected a duty nor spoke an untruth, when I informed the Lieutenant-colonel, in the first instance by word of mouth, and afterwards by letter, that I had complied with his order. It will have been shown from the cross-examination of Lieutenant and Adjutant Hecker, that I received a verbal communication from him to the effect, that captains of troops were to inform their men of the praise that had, on the morning of that day, been bestowed upon the regiment by the Major-general; I accordingly went, (as has been proved,) to evening stables, to comply with this order. Finding that the orderly officer had been round before, I did not again call the men from their horses, but I mentioned in each stable the few words necessary, and which were verbatim, as stated in my letter to the Lieutenant-colonel, which has been read to the Court. Lance-Serjeant Denby has stated that I was not at stables; I purpose calling up a man from each of his stables to bear witness to my having been there, and that I spoke to them as I have stated, in compliance with his Lordship's orders, and further, that I ordered the men that were in one stable to go into the next. I trust the Court will consider that more direct and convincing evidence could not be desired, to disprove this most odious charge of having made a statement contrary to truth and fact. As I have already stated, it is much to be regretted that it should have been put forward without affording me any opportunity for explanation, and that the Lieutenant-colonel, (apparently without hesitation,) should have permitted himself to doubt my verbal and written statement.

Captain Wathen's defence.

"The next accusation is, neglect of duty; it will be seen, and the Lieutenant-colonel must have been perfectly aware at the time he put the charge upon paper, that if I had not read the order to the men on the evening in question, that I should not have neglected a duty, or disobeyed an order. His Lordship, in directing the orderly officer to read the *same* order to the men at evening stables, must be considered to have cancelled the former verbal order; and it is to be presumed that he did so, considering it would be inconvenient for the officers to leave the dinner table, at the time the Major-general did them the honour to dine at the mess. Why, therefore, with this foreknowledge, should his Lordship have singled me out as having neglected a duty, when it appears I was the only one who performed it, if it could be considered such? The Court will draw the inference, and I cannot give a stronger proof of the feeling in which the charge must have been framed.

Fifth Charge.

" 'For that he, Captain Wathen, after having assembled the men of his troop, on Saturday, 9th of November, 1833, at the place aforesaid, addressed them in an irregular and unofficerlike manner, by then and there, not confining himself to communicating to them the Major-general's approbation of the regiment, but in adding that some strangers or civilians had particularly remarked the soldier-like appearance of his troop, or words to that effect, and also saying that he had no doubt that had they gone on service, they would have done their duty as well as any other troop, notwithstanding any unpleasant circumstances which had occurred in the troop, or words to that effect; which address was highly improper, inasmuch as allusion was therein made to Lieutenant-Colonel Lord Brudenell's recent censure on the want of attention to the care of the horses in Captain Wathen's troop.'

" It appears to me that this fifth charge might be answered in a few sentences, and that it would not be absolutely necessary, in order to exculpate myself, to call upon any further witnesses than those who have been brought forward by the prosecutor with a contrary intention. But it is absolutely necessary to my defence, (the more particularly regarding the sixth charge, where I am accused, in two instances, of disobedience of orders,) to show the disposition, by which I had reason to believe the Lieutenant-colonel was actuated towards me, as it was in consequence of such an impression on my part, that my conduct was influenced, in declining to comply with the commands of the Lieutenant-colonel. For this reason, and for my more ample justification, it is necessary that I should bring all the circumstances connected with the present charge, under the notice of the Court. I trust it will be found, upon examination, that the grounds upon which this charge is preferred, are as untenable, as, I imagine it must have appeared to the Court, were those of the former, upon which I have closed my defence. If such shall appear to be the case, it will be evident that the prosecutor could only have been influenced, in bringing it forward, by a similar feeling to that which must have guided him in the other numerous instances to which I have already, and shall still have occasion to refer: nothing but such feelings could have led the prosecutor for a moment to suppose, that I might, or could, have been guilty of the folly and wickedness with which he now charges me, by setting forth, that it was my intention, upon the occasion alluded to, to place the conduct of my commanding-officer in an improper light, in the eyes of the troop. The slightest reflection would have taught him, that it was impossible that I could be guilty, and I humbly conceive might also have made him sensible, that it was utterly inconsistent with his own credit and position, to entertain and act upon suspicions so injurious to the honour, sense, and character, of any officer under his command. I need not state to the officers of this honourable Court, that the tenor of a captain's commission, enjoins that 'he should use his best endeavours to preserve good order and discipline in his troop.' The usages of the service permit, that when occasion requires, he should address his men, and explain any points of duty which he may consider to require their attention, and by a few words of commendation or censure, endeavour to ensure a willing obedience to his commands. My having done this, and I shall be enabled to show that I did nothing more, has been represented as an offence committed on my part, and is now charged against

Captain Wathen's defence.

me as a crime. I shall, therefore, proceed to bring the facts under the notice of the Court. Information is taken to the Lieutenant-colonel, that Captain Wathen had addressed his men *at night*. What are the steps pursued by the Lieutenant-colonel? does he reprove the tale bearer, and thus discourage a practice so revolting to those honourable feelings, which should exist in the bosom of a soldier, or does he, at the least, send for the officer at once, and charge him with having taken a step, which he, the Lieutenant-colonel, considers to be improper? His Lordship did not pursue either of these courses. He sent for a lance, or acting serjeant, whom, judging by experience on a former occasion, he had reason to suppose was badly affected towards his captain. He singled this man out from a whole troop, to give him information as to what had passed, and a statement was drawn up. The Lieutenant-colonel then sent for my troop serjeant-major. This non-commissioned officer he questions and cross-questions, examines and re-examines, and in the presence of the *lance serjeant* and the *adjutant*, as witnesses, his words are noted down, and he is at last called upon to sign a statement, which is drawn up for him by the adjutant, and with the contents of which the Court have been enabled to perceive that he was indifferently acquainted.

" These were the preliminary steps adopted by the Lieutenant-colonel, which in the event of my having been really guilty of the improper conduct he was willing to attribute to me, ought surely to have been a reason to induce his Lordship to act with caution in so delicate an affair, to which it would have been dangerous and improper to draw the attention and excite the suspicions of private soldiers. After these men had been examined, and not until the third day after my alleged offence was committed, *I* was sent

Captain Wathen's defence.

for, and what passed between us has been already described. I imagine it must appear that the proceedings which then took place, were as illegal as they were ungenerous and unjust, and in opposition to the rules of the service. The next act of the Lieutenant-colonel was to call up the remaining non-commissioned officers presen twith my troop, and to proceed in a similar manner to that which he had adopted towards the others, and to the captain of the troop to which they belonged. Is it to be wondered at that soldiers, under these circumstances, should sign papers with the real meaning and intent of which they were doubtful? Those who have been long subject to military discipline, can alone be aware of the trying position in which those non-commissioned officers were placed when interrogated and confused by the authority of the Lieutenant-colonel commanding their regiment. It has appeared, from the examination of these non-commissioned officers, that they were, upon various occasions, called up to be interrogated as to the conduct of the captain of their troop, and were examined, both separately and in presence of Lance-serjeant Denby and the adjutant. I must appeal to the Court if any evidence that has been produced in regard to my alleged misconduct could have warranted such a proceeding on the part of the Lieutenant-colonel. I feel sure that neither the character he has heard of me from other superior officers, or my conduct in regard to himself, since he has had command of the regiment, could have warranted him, or in any manner have borne him out, in forming such suspicions, or in resorting to such harsh measures on my account, which it was apparent must prove so injurious to my character in the regiment, and must tend to lessen my influence and control over those whom it was my duty, (under the authority of

Captain Wathen's defence.

the Lieutenant-colonel,) to command. I have stated, and it has been shown in evidence by the witnesses brought forward on the part of the prosecution, that it was a regimental custom for captains of troops to address their men; that this circumstance was known to the Lieutenant-colonel; that he had himself been in the habit of directing officers commanding troops to speak to their men; and that he had even desired that I would make a verbal communication to the men of my troop, on the night preceding the morning on which I had again spoken to them, and which is now made the substance of the present charge. Under these circumstances I appeal to this honourable Court, whether, therefore, the mere act of my addressing my troop can be urged against me. I feel confident that their decision on this question will be in my favour; it will therefore only be necessary for me to consider the *matter* contained in the few words that I addressed to the non-commissioned officers and men of my troop. After having diligently searched my memory, it appears to me, that what I stated to the Lieutenant-colonel verbally, and also in my letter to him, contains the whole substance of what I said to my men, and I cannot find I have omitted any particular. In considering these few sentences, I do not find, on comparing them with the evidence brought forward by the prosecutor, with a view of invalidating the correctness of my statement, that any thing has been adduced, that does not tend to corroborate it, as a correct report of what I said. The substance given by his witnesses is the same, although the words may differ, which is natural. The whole of the evidence drawn from these witnesses by Lord Brudenell, only goes to prove the accuracy of the report I had already made to the Lieutenant-colonel upon the subject of what I had said to my troop, and which I had immediately volunteered to put down for him in writing; it will be observed, that the Lieutenant-colonel has endeavoured to show that the displeasure expressed by me to my men, related to his own conduct; but I have shown that the cause for my assembling them, was the circumstance of *their* having *displeased me* on that very morning. The feelings in his Lordship's own breast, and his consciousness of the measures he had pursued towards me, might have made *him* entertain such suspicions, on hearing what had been reported to him; but I do not think there is one amongst them, *who, if left to himself,* would have drawn any such inference from what I said, as has been implied in the charge; and indeed it has been clearly proved that they did not. The *intent* which led me to speak to the men, may be clearly ascertained from the words used in the first sentence, which was uttered by me, wherein I point out that I considered that the men had been remiss, and give an especial reason why they should not have been so. If I was really anxious as to their good behaviour, could I have taken any other method, either ostensible, or, in fact, which was better calculated to stimulate them to leave no opening for fault being found, than to address them in the manner I did? I appeal to the Court whether a sufficient cause for my so addressing them is not to be found in my anxiety for their good appearance and conduct, at a moment when the Major-general was about to conclude his inspection of the regiment; without (as in the case of the Lieutenant-colonel) going out of the way in order to find a *particular* reason for my having done that which was only usual, and thus drawing inferences so injurious as those contained in the charge, which the evidence that has been adduced by no

Captain Wathen's defence.

means warranted. I may next inquire, and I put it to the consideration of the Court, on the supposition that I had had an intention of making any statement which I did not consider myself authorized to make, whether it was probable that I should have fixed upon the period of the *mid-day* stable hour for doing so, and have chosen for my place of assembly, a stable nearly opposite the *regimental office* with the door open; more particularly, as I was aware from past occurrences, that my conduct was watched, and that any circumstances which could be turned in any way to my disadvantage, would be taken notice of. If it was considered I had committed myself, why was it allowed to remain uninquired into from Saturday noon till Tuesday afternoon? The Court will observe that the Lieutenant-colonel never inquired of me what my intention in addressing my men was, nor did he even ask (as it is but natural to expect he should have done) if I intended to allude to the censure he refers to; on the contrary, he never gave me an opportunity to undeceive him, nor did I ever know of his ill-grounded suspicions till furnished with my charges.

"I feel that these are circumstances which must weigh with the Court, and that taking every thing into consideration, they will also upon this charge grant me an honourable acquittal; and as in the former case, I must again remark, that had there been any consideration on the part of the Lieutenant-colonel, it must have prevented his ever having put it forward against me.

Sixth Charge.

"'For having on the 12th of November, 1833, at the place aforesaid, refused to obey an order then given to him by Lieutenant-colonel Lord Brudenell, his commanding officer to repeat verbally what he had said to his men on the said Saturday, the 9th of November, and in having afterwards, when permitted by his said commanding officer, to commit to writing the nature of the said address to his troop, repeatedly refused to obey the order then and there verbally given to him by his said commanding officer, to leave his written statement locked up in the regimental office during his absence on parade. Such conduct as aforesaid being insubordinate, unbecoming the character of an officer and a gentleman, to the prejudice of good order and military discipline, and a breach of the Articles of War.'

Captain Wathen's defence.

" I have already pressed upon the attention of the Court the singular circumstance that this charge, the sixth, which is of a very serious nature, being for repeated disobedience of orders, and moreover the cause of my being placed in arrest, should be the last mentioned, and that charge, which has been the least dwelt upon in the prosecution. But there is another circumstance connected with this charge, which, being an isolated transaction, has not been adverted to in the relation of events which I, in the first instance, made to the Court, in the order in which they occurred; but which, as it strongly bears upon the circumstances of the case, must not be omitted.

" On the evening of the 10th of November, Major Sir Walter Scott was put in orders as president of a regimental Court-Martial, when it was my turn of duty. On inquiry of Sir Walter Scott, why I was put out of my turn, he mentioned the reason which his Lordship assigned for so doing, and which has already been explained to the Court. If his Lordship entertained this opinion of the excited state of my mind, I may ask if it can be considered reasonable in him, that he should have endeavoured to

Captain Wathen's defence.

cause me to make a hurried statement of transactions to which he appeared to attach great importance, and should then endeavour to obtain such statement, before I had possessed myself of a copy of it, or had even finished it, or read over what I had written? Lord Brudenell, from what he had said to Major Sir Walter Scott, wished to make it understood, that my mind was in a state of agitation. It appears to me that his Lordship in this matter has, (to say the least of it,) pursued a very inconsistent course. He affirms that Captain Wathen's mind is in an unusual state of agitation; be it so.—Who, then, if it was so, brought about such a state? The answer is obvious,—the prosecutor! for as no one else observed any thing unusual in me, it must have been only in his imagination; and if in the prosecutor's imagination, he must have felt self-accused, and perhaps conceived that by the line of conduct he had adopted towards me, he had given me cause to be in such a state of mind as he implied; but the prosecutor did not allow that state of agitation to interfere with the examination I underwent by the general on Monday, (the 11th of November,) the very day the Court-Martial was held; and on the following day also, he forgets these fears of my not being equal to my duty, and calls *me*, the person who was reduced to such an agitated and excited state of mind, as not to be able to sit president of a regimental Court-Martial, to undergo a close cross-examination on a subject on which the prosecutor was well acquainted, and I unprepared, he having already cross-examined on it two non-commissioned officers. From their evidence the adjutant had drawn up a statement which was the groundwork of my own examination, at a time too, when the trumpets were sounding for parade for a corporal punishment, which, of course, was a reason to be hurried in the arrangement of ideas, and afforded the prosecutor an excuse for so hurrying me, of which he did not neglect to avail himself. If the assertion, that I was in an agitated state of mind was correct, the onus of it must rest with his Lordship, for he not only proves by it his own unkindness, but also a wish to procure *information* from me whilst under such influence; certainly this was not a generous proceeding; if I was not fit for one duty, I was not fit for the other, or equal to undergo a close examination on a matter I had dismissed from my mind, the occurrence in question having taken place three days previously; but on this point I shall not dwell at greater length, leaving the Court to draw such inferences as are inseparable from the facts now stated.

Captain Wathen's defence.

"I now proceed to the consideration of the charge itself. The first crime of which I am accused, (for disobedience of orders must be termed by this harsh epithet, however grating it may sound to the ears of an officer, who for the first time stands in a position to be so arraigned,) is for having refused to repeat verbally, to the Lieutenant-colonel, what I had said to my men. It appears to me that any person unacquainted with the circumstances which have been brought before the Court, would suppose from the wording of this part of the charge, that I declined verbally communicating to him what I had said to my men; but it appears that I am only accused of having declined to state over again verbally, what I had already related, and I have no wish to disprove the circumstance. My words had been already noted down, and if they were to be committed to paper (as I could not doubt with a view of being afterwards produced against me,) I thought I might at least request the privilege of writing them myself. I offered to commit to writing what I had said, but I declined again verbally to repeat it, under the circumstances in which I

Captain Wathen's defence.

was situated; I considered the command an unlawful one, and I felt that it could have been given with no other motive than a view of endeavouring to turn any trifling difference of expression to my disadvantage. I therefore preferred giving my statement in writing. In the second part of the charge I am accused of disobedience of orders in repeatedly refusing to leave a written statement locked up in the regimental office during my absence on parade. There are two grounds upon which I may urge objections to this part of the charge: first, I do not acknowledge that the paper alluded to was a *statement;* being *unfinished, unsigned*, and consequently *unauthorized* as a relation of facts, it cannot, I think, strictly speaking, be so termed. As a statement or document, it was a valueless piece of paper, although it might have been made disadvantageous to me.

"The second objection to its validity, is the same which I have already urged to the first part of the charge, viz. that I do not consider the order to have been a lawful one, or in consonance with the usages of his Majesty's service. My reasons for not giving up the paper on which I had written, are as follow:—

"1st. I conceive that any composition of my own is my private property, and that it continues to be my own until I voluntarily deliver it into the hands of the person for whom it is intended, when it becomes his, and I have no further controul over it.

"2dly. I am not willing to give another person controul over my writings till I have thoroughly and leisurely corrected, revised, copied, and signed them, none of which was I allowed time to do, or could do, when they were demanded from me; and as I had every reason to believe that I should, as far as possible, have been made accountable for every word of these writings, for omissions, and for any inadvertencies which they might contain, I could not have given them up until such had been corrected. An accidental omission might have been held to be a wilful one, and I might have suffered for it; it would or might have been urged that they were my own words, and that I was not authorized in withdrawing them or substituting others.

Captain Wathen's defence.

"3dly. As the commanding officer employed *an officer* of the regiment to take down my words in the regimental office, and, *unknown to me*, to keep a memorandum of what I had said, I therefore on no account would have omitted to take a copy of any statement which I might make in writing, and I consider that every individual, whether in his Majesty's service or not, is entitled to this self-protection. I conceive that the Lieutenant-colonel would have been as much justified in ordering me to deliver to him a private letter, as an unfinished, imperfect, and unrevised document of my own, in the composition of which it must be supposed that every officer is at liberty, before delivering it, to take his own time, and not to be hurried in such a manner as to afford a great probability that he would write something which he would alter, on referring to, and which, if unaltered, might, from its being written in the hurry of the moment, be liable seriously to commit him. The Lieutenant-colonel has admitted that if in what he should elicit he found grounds for accusation, that it was at that time his intention to prefer charges against me: it is therefore manifest that in demanding from me this hurried statement he was endeavouring to induce me to do that which might criminate myself, and if such a procedure is illegal, it follows that his Lordship's command, that I should give up the paper, was also unlawful. I must also ask what reason had his Lordship for wishing to possess himself *instantaneously* of my unfinished statement? If his Lordship states that I ought to have given the paper up when he engaged to lock it up, and that neither the ad-

Captain Wathen's defence.

jutant or himself should see it, I say that I resist the principle of giving up what is my own. The Lieutenant-colonel was then trying to make second terms with me. Of what advantage could it be to the Lieutenant-colonel to possess the paper, if he did not originally intend to look at it? He admitted that he ought not to look at it. What right had I to place more confidence in him and his Lordship's adjutant, than he manifested towards me? On the contrary, had I not every reason to be cautious, after the discovery made of the secret arrangement to note in writing what I said? I *can* only account for his desire to possess it by the supposition that he would have looked at it, and made me answerable for its contents, or at least might have taken such advantage as could be derived from the knowledge of any circumstance that had been inadvertently put down, *and all this at a time when his Lordship affected to be under an impression* that my mind was in such a state of excitement as to unfit me for regimental duty. Had his Lordship not been so eager to place me under arrest, I should, in all probability, have allowed myself to be guided by the judgment of a senior officer, and if Sir Walter Scott had recommended me to give up the paper, (had I been permitted time to consider,) I think his opinion might have induced me to do so, which would have obviated any occasion for preferring against me the present charges; but it will be observed, Lord Brudenell having ascertained (from a mere sentence uttered by Sir Walter Scott) what he supposed to be that officer's opinion, took advantage of it himself, as he considered that it confirmed his own view of the subject; but he was determined I should not avail myself of it, in order to rectify the error he supposed I had committed, and his Lordship therefore cut the matter short, by saying it was too late, and forthwith quitting the office.

"I trust I may now have shown that the grounds upon which the charge is formed are untenable, and I am induced to hope that the Court will grant me that full and honourable acquittal I feel myself deserving of.

Captain Wathen's defence.

"I have now been under arrest for the space of nine weeks; upon the former occasion I was confined within the barrack walls for one month: the suspense and anxiety which must naturally be felt by any officer during the period charges are pending against him, was experienced by me to the full extent; I might, at least, have hoped to be freed from any other vexation; but I did not even then escape annoyance. I should not now have made any reference to this subject, had not the Lieutenant-colonel himself reminded me of it, in a very unpleasant manner, by sending the adjutant to me, when I had chanced to be accosted by a friend, to desire that I would not walk or associate with officers. With charges pending against me, I cannot but consider that the debarring me from free intercourse with my friends was, at least, an ungenerous proceeding; but I made no objection, and I have since abstained, as much as possible, from walking with any of my military acquaintances.

"It is well understood, that commanding officers are vested with discretionary powers in regard to placing their officers under arrest; but I believe they are seldom exerted to their full extent, and that an officer is not generally confined to his room and debarred communication with his friends, previous to his trial, unless it is considered that his offence is of an ungentlemanly or very grave nature. Upon the former occasion, as well as upon the present, I was at first strictly confined to my room, and I consider that an unfavourable impression might consequently have

Captain Wathen's defence.

been made in the garrison in regard to me, from observing that the commanding officer appeared to think that my conduct rendered such strong measures necessary.

"I shall now mention another circumstance, which evinces the system of 'espionage,' to which I have before alluded, was continued. One morning I walked round by the guard-house, and immediately returned. Lord Brudenell, who was in the barrack-yard, appeared to observe my going towards the gate. The building having possibly hid me for a time from his view, Lord Brudenell *went himself* to the serjeant, and inquired 'If Captain Wathen *had gone out* of the gate,' and was answered in the negative. Had I done so, it must be inferred, that his Lordship would have considered that I had broken my arrest.

"I have now terminated all those remarks which appear necessary to defend myself from the charges preferred against me, and it only remains for me to call such evidence as may be still considered wanting in the statements I have urged in my defence. I believe that this is the proper time to bring under the notice of the Court, any testimonials I may possess, of a favourable nature; I therefore have the honour to submit for perusal, some original letters with which I have been favoured, and as they refer to my conduct, during nearly the whole period from the commencement of my military service until the present time, I trust that the Court will be inclined to take them into its favourable consideration, in deciding upon my cause. I must request the indulgence of the Court, for detaining them upon such a subject. I cannot but feel, that in comparison with the gallant services and arduous duties which have been performed by the distinguished officers to whom I now address myself, that my own service is but of small importance, nor, indeed would it ever have been referred to by me, and more particularly in so public a manner, did I not conceive it was necessary to my defence.

Captain Wathen's defence.

"I have held his Majesty's commission for twenty years, and although I commenced my service in a civil department of the army, I must, as a soldier, look back to that period with satisfaction. I served two active campaigns, and in the year 1815, being at Brussels, I had the advantage of witnessing the operations of the armies on the 16th and 17th, and was present at Waterloo, on the 18th of June.

"It will be seen from the testimony of Lieutenant-General Sir Colquhoun Grant, the *present colonel of the regiment*, under whose immediate command I served in Dublin, as also of Major-General Sir John Browne, and Colonel Thackwell, my former commanding officer, that they had reason to be perfectly satisfied with my conduct during a period of many years. Lieutenant-Colonel Lord Brudenell has been in command of the regiment not quite two years, and this is the second occasion within a month on which he has preferred charges against me. I cannot, therefore, but feel that I have met with much unkindness, where I might naturally have looked for protection and support; but I have endeavoured, throughout the transactions which have taken place, to conduct myself with temperance and forbearance, and I now entertain a confident hope, that it will appear to the Court that I am not guilty upon any of the charges. I have now but few remaining words to offer, and in closing my remarks, I trust I may be excused if I give utterance to those feelings of grateful acknowledgment with which I am sensibly impressed, for the patient hearing and impartial investigation, which has been afforded to me during this trial. May I, therefore,

Captain Wathen's defence.

be permitted to return my thanks for this, not only to the president and members severally, composing this honourable Court, but also to his Majesty's Deputy Judge Advocate-General. I have the satisfaction of knowing that my cause is under the consideration of officers, who, from long years of military experience, must be competent to decide upon it, and this reflection has been a source of comfort to me, throughout the suspense and anxiety which I have suffered during the long period of my arrest.

"My labours are now nearly completed, and I finally commit my defence into the hands of this honourable Court, under the full conviction, that, be their decision what it may, that it will be founded in justice, and in accordance with the rules of the service, to which I have the honour to belong.

"A. Wathen,
Captain 15th King's Hussars.

"*Cork Barracks*,
13*th January*, 1834."

Major Sir Walter Scott's evidence.

Major Sir Walter Scott, of the 15th Hussars, was recalled; and, having been already sworn, was cross-examined by the Prisoner, on the charges generally.

Q. In the mess-room, on the 20th of October, when Lord Hill's decision was read, do you remember any observation made by Lord Brudenell, in regard to Lord Hill's opinion about the trumpet sounds?

A. There was an observation, but at this moment I do not recollect the purport of it.

Q. During the time I was under arrest on a former occasion, did you consider that my troop improved or appeared better managed than when I was in command of it? Major Sir Walter Scott's evidence.

A. Certainly not.

Q. Did I not, on Thursday, the 7th of November, mention to you that I had just quitted the regimental office, and that the Lieutenant-colonel had found much fault with me on account of the excess of debt of my troop, and that he said I should have to account for it to the major-general?

A. Yes.

Q. Do you consider the issues of stable-jackets and cloth overalls, which have lately been made in this regiment, to be unusual issues?

A. Certainly, with regard to jackets.

Q. At the foot parade on the 11th of November, do you recollect private Hopkins's jacket being produced to the Major-general; and when the subject was discussed, how did the Lieutenant-colonel dispose of the jacket?

A. He threw it away.

Q. From your knowledge of me during the nine years I have been under your personal observation, do you consider me capable of wilfully making any assertion or statement contrary to truth and fact; or of making an invidious representation to the inspecting general or any other authority?

A. Most certainly not.

Q. Be so good as to state to the Court what occurred at the dismounted parade a few days previous to the inspection of the 8th of November, when some of the men were discontented at being charged with the crosses for their arms, when sent to punishment drill, in consequence of their horses having sore backs?

A. Lieutenant-Colonel Lord Brudenell addressed the

Major Sir Walter Scott's evidence.

men, pointing out to them how highly disreputable the number of sore backs in the regiment would appear, should it ever become known to any other cavalry corps; that they would become the laughing-stock of any regiment they might be quartered with, and further, that this fact would probably be made known to the major-general at the approaching inspection, in consequence of some men refusing to sign their accounts, as they had been charged in their accounts with green crosses, for giving their horses sore backs; that he had no doubt that the good old soldiers of the regiment, to save the regiment that disgrace, would subscribe their pence and halfpence to pay for those crosses, and that he trusted it would be kept a regimental secret.

Q. Were the horses in fair condition when the regiment arrived at Newbridge, and low in flesh, and poor and weakly when they quitted the quarters for Kilkenny and Carlow?

A. No regiment ever marched into Newbridge in better condition. I never saw such a squadron as I had the command of when I left Newbridge, in regard to their low condition, and number of sore backs.

Q. Will you mention the number of field days and skirmishing drills per week, during the period the regiment was stationed at Newbridge, the general pace of movement, the length of the drills, and the number of hours the horses were mounted, from the first turn out till the return of the regiment to barracks, and how long they were generally saddled?

A. I was there seven weeks; for the first five weeks, we certainly were out four times each week, the other two weeks three times each week, in mounting and skirmishing drills; the general pace of movement at field days was a trot of eight miles an hour, wheeling at the gallop—from the time the men turned out until we returned to barracks, five hours; if we came in warm, the horses were saddled two hours.

Major Sir Walter Scott's evidence.

Q. Was the same system of drill which you have described at Newbridge, resumed in these quarters; and did not six or seven horses come down at one field day—and do you ascribe their falling to their being at the time weak and unequal to the work?

A. The system of drill was not to the same extent in these quarters. I average the number of field days in Cork, from one inspection to the other, at three per week; and the time occupied four hours and a half, from turn out. Five horses came down one field day in my own squadron, but whether they fell from the length of the day's work, or from weakness, it would be hard to describe.

Q. Are you of opinion that the horses that had sore backs were allowed time for recovery, or were they continued in the ranks at field days and drills at Newbridge, or again since our arrival at Cork?

A. I don't know.

[It being four o'clock, the Court adjourned until eleven o'clock the following morning.]

Tuesday, January 14.

The Court met pursuant to adjournment, with the exception of Major Mitchell, still absent from indisposition.

Major Sir Walter Scott was recalled, and examined by the Prosecutor, through the Court.

Q. By the Prosecutor, through the Court.—State to the Court to what cause you attribute there having been only

Major Sir Walter Scott's evidence.

one sore-backed horse in Captain Blyth's troop, two in Captain Macqueen's, and five in Captain Rose's troop since we left Dublin, since which there have been twenty-three in Captain Wathen's troop?

A. I doubt the accuracy of the return, knowing that in other troops there have been thirteen sore backs at one time—many officers not considering that to be a sore back which others would. Captains Blyth and Macqueen's troop did not come under my observation.

Q. After I had appealed to the officers for their co-operation and assistance, together with other measures, which I thought proper to adopt, were not the irregularities with regard to sore backs completely checked shortly previous to the inspection in all the troops, except Captain Wathen's, without the drills and field days being in any degree diminished?

A. Captain Wathen's troop, and that of another officer, was put in orders, the sore backs being greater in number in these troops than in any other. The horses in the one troop recovered sooner than those in Captain Wathen's; but there may have been more severe cases in Captain Wathen's, until the 8th of November, when we were inspected. The same drills and field days took place.

Q. At several watering parades previous to the inspection, were there not at least six or seven horses brought to parade in Captain Wathen's troop with sore backs, when there was only one other sore-backed horse in the regiment?

A. I do not recollect such a proportion.

Q. By the Court. Do you consider, from every thing that came under your observation as the senior major of the regiment, that Captain Wathen, being several weeks under arrest, relieved him from the responsibility of any irregularities which may have occurred in his troop during that period, and for some time after?

Major Sir Walter Scott's evidence.

A. During the period Captain Wathen was in arrest, he was completely absolved from all responsibility. On resuming the command, had he found any ground for complaint, he should have made a report of it to the commanding officer.

Q. Did you see any difference between any service troops of the 15th Hussars as to discipline and appearance; and if so, state in what troop or troops this difference existed?

A. I can draw no distinction between the service troops.

Major Courtney Philipps, of the 15th Hussars, was duly sworn, and examined on the charges generally.

Major Courtney Philipps' evidence.

Q. While under your command at Carlow, state to the Court your opinion of my troop as to grooming; and also as to my zeal and attention as an officer?

A. I was perfectly satisfied with the grooming of Captain Wathen's troop when under my command at Carlow; I always found him, when there, most zealous and attentive to his duty.

Q. What was apparent on the horses' backs in the squadron at Carlow, after the march from Newbridge?

A. An unusual number of horses of the squadron were more or less injured on their backs.

Q. Did you mention the circumstance to his Lordship? and if so, state what passed.

A. When Lord Brudenell came to Carlow, he inquired the state of the squadron; I told him there were a great many backs injured on the march from Newbridge; his

Major Courtney Philipps' evidence.

Lordship asked me if I had sent the men to drill. I answered that I had not, that I conceived it was not the fault of the men.

Q. Did you hear any remarks made by his Lordship regarding sore backs before we left Newbridge? if so, please to state them.

A. I did, in Captain Ives' troop; his Lordship remarked in the stables, three or four times, that there were seventeen horses lame, or with sore backs.

Q. Please state the average number of hours the horses were mounted during the field days at Newbridge, from the first turn-out until the return of the regiment to barracks; and whether the field days were the only mounted duties for the horses of the regiment?

A. The average was about five hours; the field days were not the only mounted duties; there were squad drills on the other days.

Q. Have you ever found me, or observed that I have been disrespectful towards my superior officers; and from your knowledge of my character, do you suppose me capable of wilfully making a misrepresentation?

A. I have never observed Captain Wathen disrespectful to his superior officers; and I consider him incapable of wilfully making a misrepresentation.

Cross-examination.

Q. Immediately previous to marching into these quarters, had not the troops been at out-quarters for six weeks; and had there been any drills or other work for the troop horses during that time?

A. They were at out-quarters for about six weeks: the squadron at Carlow under my command had had drills three times in the week.

Q. With reference to the length of field days, what was the usual length of time when the regiment was quartered at Hounslow under Colonel Thackwell; and what number of hours was the Hampton Court squadron usually kept out? **Major Courtney Philipps' evidence.**

A. To the best of my recollection, the troops at Hounslow about five hours; at Hampton Court rather more than two hours and twenty minutes longer.

Q. Are not the mounted duties of the regiment the same now as they were at that time?

A. As to length or numbers they are.

Q. Have you reason to believe that there ever were in those days the same number of sore backs which have existed last year?

A. I do not recollect any thing like the number.

Q. Did not Colonel Thackwell invariably send men to drill who had given their horses sore backs?

A. If Colonel Thackwell conceived it was the fault of the man, he was invariably sent to drill.

Q. *By the Court.* Why did you consider that it was not the men's fault that their horses' backs were sore; and to what cause did you attribute the great number of sore backs in the King's Hussars?

A. I conceive it was not the fault of the men, as those horses that were injured, their saddle-trees did not fit them, from their low condition.

Q. Since the 15th Hussars have been in Ireland, have any of the horses with sore backs been worked in the ranks before their backs were perfectly well?

A. Not to my knowledge.

Q. What is the usual length of field days in the cavalry, as far as you are conversant with the custom of the service?

A. I can't answer that question.

Serjeant-Major Thom's evidence.

Serjeant-Major Thom, of Captain Wathen's troop, was recalled, and being already sworn, was examined.

Q. Name the men in my troop whose horses were worked in the ranks before their backs were perfectly well.

A. Privates Surrett, Stretch, Barret, Peacock, Johnson, Carter, Roberts.

Q. On the arrival of my troop in the barracks, did I not make out, from a minute and personal inspection, a list of the trees which appeared to pinch the horses' backs, and press upon the withers?

A. Yes.

Q. State what the Lieutenant-colonel informed you, the veterinary surgeon had told him relative to the sore backs in all troops but mine?

A. Lieutenant-Colonel Lord Brudenell told me that he was assured by the veterinary surgeon, about the 26th of November, that there was but one case of bad back in the three troops then stationed at Cork, with the exception of Captain Wathen's troop. At the same time I was aware that there were three or four cases of bad backs in the service troop of Captain Ives.

Q *By the Prosecutor, through the Court.* Were not all the saddle-trees fitted under my own superintendence, after we marched into these barracks?

A. I cannot speak positively to any; but generally they were.

Q. Did I not say that I ordered so many saddle-trees to be repaired and altered, as a precautionary measure, before going on foreign service; and that many of such repairs were unnecessary for home service, particularly the number of forks repaired?

A. I do not recollect the words.

Serjeant-Major Thom's evidence.

Q. By whose orders were these horses worked in the ranks, with sore backs?

A. The veterinary surgeon.

Captain Rose, of the 15th Hussars, being already sworn, was cross-examined by the prisoner on all the charges generally.

Captain Rose's evidence.

Q. When the major-general asked you in the orderly-room, on the 8th of November, if the issue of stable-jackets to your troops was an unusual one, what was your reply?

A. I was not aware that it was.

Q. When explaining to the major-general that he had misconceived my words, did I not entreat him to remember my words, that I had said I heard it from my serjeant, my serjeant-major, he being my clerk, and that therefore it was natural he should explain the cause of my troop debt?

A. Yes.

Q. Did the major-general ever say in your presence that my conduct was insubordinate; and do you think me capable of wilfully making a mis-statement?

A. As to the first part of the question, I heard nothing of the sort. I do not think you capable of wilfully making a mis-statement.

Q. Did I call the major-general's attention to the conduct of Lord Brudenell towards me in his Lordship's presence? and what observation did the major-general make in reply?

A. Captain Wathen was proceeding to detail to the major-general what he conceived to be grievances which he had received at the hands of Lord Brudenell, when the

Captain Rose's evidence.

major-general requested him to abstain for the present from this course, as he was then merely investigating matters of finance.

Q. By the Prosecutor, through the Court.—Did not the circumstance of this alleged conversation occur after a parade, under arms, on Friday, the 8th of November?

A. I quite forget whether it was before or after; I rather think it was after, but I cannot swear to it.

Q. Was it not dark when the major-general left the orderly-room, immediately after this conversation?

A. It was dark.

Troop Serjeant Major John Leech's evidence.

Troop Serjeant-Major John Leech, of the 15th Hussars, and of Captain Wathen's troop, was duly sworn and examined on the charges generally.

Q. Was private Ambrose's horse reported for having a sore back at Cork, or was he only returned as sick by the veterinary surgeon?

A. He was only returned sick; he had a sore back.

Q. What orders have you received from the regimental office about charging the jackets to the men, and have they been all charged? if not, state the reason.

A. I don't recollect the receiving any orders from the regimental office; but from Captain Ives I received directions not to charge them until the month of December, and they were all charged in that month.

Serjeant Clarkson's evidence.

Serjeant Clarkson, of the 15th Hussars, being already sworn, was cross-examined.

Q. Was I at evening stables on the 8th of November,

and did I speak to the men of your squad relative to what the major-general had said? Serjeant Clarkson's evidence.

A. Yes, you did speak to the men.

Q. How many stables can you answer for as to Captain Wathen's having spoken to his men?

A. Two.

Private Robert Young, of the 15th Hussars, of Captain Wathen's troop, was duly sworn and examined. Private Rob. Young's evidence.

Q. Are you in Serjeant Denby's squad; and did I speak to the men at stables on Friday evening, the 8th of November, relative to the praise bestowed on the regiment by the major-general?

A. I am in Serjeant Denby's squad. Yes, you did.

Q. Has Captain Wathen, or any person by his order, lately questioned you, or spoken to you about what you would have to say before the Court Martial?

A. No one.

Lieutenant-Colonel Chatterton, of the 4th Dragoon Guards, a member of the Court, was duly sworn and examined as to the general character of the prisoner. Lieutenant-Colonel Chatterton's evidence.

Q. Be good enough to state to the Court how long you have known me, and what your opinion is of my character as an officer and a gentleman.

A. I have known Captain Wathen nine years, and have always heard he was particularly zealous, active, intelligent, and fond of his profession; and I am convinced from my personal knowledge of him, he would not in any way derogate from the character of an officer and a man of honour.

Testimonials. [The prisoner then handed in the different returns alluded to in his address, and produced to the Court several letters as to character. Copies of which are appended to these proceedings; he then closed his Defence.]

TESTIMONIALS TO CHARACTER.

Letter from Lieutenant-General Sir Colquhoun Grant, authorizing Captain Wathen to use his letter, dated the 12th October, 1833.

(Copy.)

Frampton, Dorsetshire,
8th Dec. 1833.

Dear Capt. Wathen,

Your letter of the 29th of November, followed me from London to this place; you have my full permission to make any use of the testimony with which I furnished you some short time since, containing my opinion of your character and conduct as an officer and a gentleman. I have nothing to add to that document, and certainly nothing to retract.

Believe me,

Faithfully yours,

(Signed) Cn. Grant.

To Captain Wathen, 15th King's Hussars.

Letter from Major-General Sir John Browne, authorizing Captain Wathen to use his letter, dated October the 3rd, 1833. Testimonials.

(Copy.)

Bromley, 8*th Dec.* 1833.

My dear Wathen,

You have my free consent to use my letter, which was written under every feeling of wishing to serve so meritorions an officer and gentleman.

I again certify the sentiments it expressed to be perfectly in unison with my invariable opinion of you.

Lady B. unites with me in very kind remembrance of you, and in requesting our respects may be offered to Lady Elizabeth Wathen.

Ever yours faithfully,
(Signed) J. Browne.

Letter from Lieutenant-Colonel Thackwell, authorizing Captain Wathen to use his letter, dated 10*th September*, 1833.

Copy.)

Roche Mount, 29*th Dec.* 1833.

Dear Wathen,

As I am sure you will be desirous, in your defence, of laying before the Court-Martial the opinion of your late commanding officer, relative to your conduct as an officer and a gentleman during the time you served under his command, I beg you will use the testimonials I gave you some time back, in any way you may judge most serviceable, and I sincerely hope it may impress a favourable opinion of the propriety, zeal, and attention manifested by you in the fulfilment of your regimental duties, and I ven-

Testimonials. ture to hope I may be permitted to add, that when I had the pleasure of meeting with you at Berlin, in 1823, I was particularly struck with the anxious manner in which you endeavoured to acquire information from the manœuvres of the Russian troops, as well as their interior management, and with this impression I had the satisfaction of recommending you to his Royal Highness the Duke of Cumberland.

Believe me, dear Wathen,

Always yours most faithfully,

(Signed) Jos. Thackwell,

Late Lt.-Col. Com. 15th King's Hussars.

To Captain Wathen, 15*th King's Hussars.*

Letter from Lieutenant-General Sir Colquhoun Grant, G.C.B. Colonel 15*th King's Hussars.*

(Copy.)

9, *Grosvenor Square,*

12*th Oct.* 1833.

Sir,

In reply to your letter of the 6th instant, only now received, I beg to state that, during the various periods you served under my command, your conduct as an officer and a gentleman claimed and obtained my entire approbation. I have had frequent occasion of noticing with praise your ability in the field, as well as your unwearied zeal in the discharge of your duties in quarters.

I have the honour to be,

Sir,

Your most obedient humble servant,

Cn. Grant, Lt.-Gen.

Col. 15th King's Hussars.

To Captain Wathen, 15*th King's Hussars.*

Letter from Lieutenant-Colonel Thackwell, late Commanding the 15th King's Hussars. Testimonials.

(Copy.)

Cork, 10*th Sept.* 1833.

DEAR WATHEN,

In compliance with your request, that I should state my opinion of your conduct as an officer and a gentleman, during the time you served under my command in the King's Hussars, I have great pleasure in saying that from the time of your joining the regiment, in 1824, to the period of my leaving it in 1832, I always found it was marked with the strictest propriety as a gentleman, and that you paid strict attention to orders in the discharge of your various duties.

Believe me, dear Wathen,
Yours, very faithfully,
JOS. THACKWELL,
Late Lieut.-Col. Comm. 15th,
or, King's Hussars.

Letter from Major-General Sir John Browne.

(Copy.)

27*th Sept.* 1826.

MY DEAR WATHEN,

I have read your promotion with much satisfaction, and offer you my sincere congratulations on it, and good wishes that it may be attended with a continuation of success, in a profession I have *always considered you a bright ornament* to.

With much haste,
Yours always,
(Signed) J. BROWNE.

Letter from Major-General Sir John Browne.

October 3, 1833.

DEAR WATHEN,

I sincerely regret your annoyance, but I feel much pleasure in meeting your requisition, and giving you the testimonials you so thoroughly deserve from me, by assuring you, that during the periods you were under *my* command, I invariably found you entitled yourself to my high opinion and valüe as an officer, (take this assertion in *all* its bearings,) and also a claimant on my regard and esteem as a gentleman and a *friend;* and when your professional views withdrew you from a continuation of service at the cavalry depôt, I much regretted it.

Believe me, my dear Wathen,
Yours truly and faithfully,
(Signed) J. BROWNE,
Major-General.

I only received your letter last evening, and immediately as possible answer it. I shall be anxious to hear of and from you.

Letter from Lieutenant-Colonel C. R. O'Donnel, late Major 15th Hussars.

(Copy.)

London, Wednesday night, Dec. 18, 1833.
1, *Union Place, Regent's Park.*

MY DEAR WATHEN,

I have this moment received your letter of the 14th instant, informing me that you are about to appear before a Court-Martial, and requesting my opinion of you as an officer and a gentleman.

It is true, the public prints have, for some time past, made me acquainted with various reports of certain unhappy differences in my old regiment, and which I have heard with much regret; but I trust they are of a nature not likely to destroy, for any period, the harmony of a corps so distinguished for its services, and for which I must ever, as one of its former members, feel no inconsiderable portion of interest and attachment. **Testimonials.**

With respect to my opinion of your character, I can with confidence assert, that during the period of the time we were brother officers in the 15th Hussars, I always had every reason to consider you, as an officer, active, zealous, intelligent, and fond of your profession, and your conduct in every respect that of a gentleman.

I am not aware of the specific charges about to be preferred against you, but I shall feel great gratification in hearing of your honourable acquittal. With best wishes for your welfare,

Believe me, my dear Wathen,
To remain very truly yours,
C. R. O'DONNEL,
Lieut. Col.; late Major 15th Hussars.

To Captain Wathen, 15th King's Hussars.

Letter from Lieutenant-Colonel M'Alpine, late Major 15th Hussars.

(Copy.)

Wynson House, Castlebar,
18th Dec. 1833.

MY DEAR SIR,

I much regret the circumstances under which you have written to me; but in reply have much pleasure in being able conscientiously to affirm, that during the time we

Testimonials. served together in the 15th Hussars, your character as an officer, a gentleman, and a man of honour, stood as high as it was possible to do. I may be allowed to add, that having an opportunity, when you were detached with me, of more particularly observing your conduct, it was such as gave me the highest satisfaction, and that your attention to your duties, and anxious desire to study and inform yourself of your profession, was unremitting; this opinion many officers at the time may have heard me express; and under present circumstances I take the liberty to repeat it, trusting that you will again be able to return satisfactorily to your duty.

I am, my dear Sir,
Very truly your's,
JAMES M'ALPINE,
Lieutenant-Colonel, late Major 15th Hussars.

Letter from Lieutenant-Colonel Byam, late Major 15th Hussars.

(Copy.)

Catesfield House, Fareham, Hants,
Dec. 20th, 1833.

SIR,

I have this moment received your letter of the 14th instant, requesting me to state my opinion of you as an officer and a gentleman, during the period I served with you in the 15th Hussars.

In reply, I have to observe, that I should be doing you little justice, did I not say that I consider your conduct, during such period, to have been perfectly unexceptionable in both particulars. As an officer, being marked by a very proper zeal and attention to your duty; and in other respects correct and honourable, living at the same time upon the best terms with your brother officers. Testimonials.

I have the honour to be, Sir,
Your very obedient, humble servant,
EDWARD BYAM,
Lt.-Col. unattached, late Major 15th Hussars.

Capt. Wathen, 15th Hussars, Cork.

Letter written by order of Lord Melbourne.

(Copy.)

Whitehall, August 4th, 1831.

SIR,

I am directed by Viscount Melbourne to acknowledge the receipt of your letter of the 3rd instant, and to express his approbation of the zeal and activity shown by you in marching so promptly with your troop to assist the civil authorities.

Lord Melbourne further desires me to thank you for your communication.

I have the honour to be, Sir,
Your obedient servant,
(Signed) JOHN PHILLIPS.

Captain Wathen, 15th King's Hussars.

Letter from Commissary-General Dunmore.

(Copy.)

Bovey Barn, Greenwich,
Dec. 11th, 1833.

MY DEAR SIR,

Your letter of the 30th ult. was forwarded to me from Harpenden, and only reached me here last night. It

Testimonials. gives me great pleasure to state my unqualified approbation of your conduct whilst acting under my orders in the commissariat department in Belgium and France; and I shall be happy to find that this record of my favourable opinion is of any use to you. I trust the steps now about to be taken will be the means of re-establishing harmony in the corps.

I remain, your's very truly,
(Signed) T. DUNMORE.

Captain Wathen, 15th Hussars, Cork.

Letter from Major Fitz-Maurice, late Rifle Brigade.
(Copy.)

Bambro', Doncaster,
Aug. 21st, 1832.

MY DEAR SIR,

I am glad to say that I have no difficulty in recollecting you at Brussels, before and after the battle of Waterloo; and also that you gave me the first information on the evening of the 18th of the arrival of the Prussians on the field, as well as of the decisive forward movement of the Duke; this is a circumstance I cannot easily forget. I recollect poor Church (who remained with me after the battle of Waterloo, being also wounded) telling me that he had talked to you for some time near the quarry in front of La Haie Sainte, about the time that one of the enemy's columns was advancing, and his giving credit to the commissary for his sang froid.

I should have answered your letter of the 18th on its arrival; but was then at the Moors, from whence I am but just returned.

I remain, my dear Sir,
Sincerely yours,
(Signed) JOHN FITZMAURICE.

Testimonial from Lieutenant-Colonel Edward Studd, late Major 15th King's Hussars. Testimonials.

(Copy.)

I hereby certify that during the time we served together in the 15th Hussars, Captain Wathen possessed and sustained the character of a gentleman, and a good and zealous officer.

(Signed) EDWARD STUDD,
Lieut.-Col. H. P. retired,

Jan. 3rd, 1834.

The Prosecutor, Lieutenant-Colonel Lord Brudenell, requested that the Court would give him one day to prepare his reply.

The Court acceded to his Lordship's request, and adjourned until eleven o'clock on the following Thursday.

Thursday, January 16.

The Court met pursuant to adjournment, with the exception of Major Mitchell, still absent from severe illness.

The Prosecutor, Lieutenant Colonel Lord Brudenell, addressed the Court as follows:—

"MR. PRESIDENT AND GENTLEMEN, Lieutenant-Colonel Lord Brudenell's reply.

"I must beg a large share of your indulgence upon the present occasion, on having so serious a task before me as to reply to the defence urged by Captain Wathen; for I here beg to observe that I have acted quite alone in this affair, and have neither consulted nor received assistance from any one individual.

"Although in the total absence of all evidence, or even attempt by the prisoner, to disprove the first three, and the

Lieutenant-Colonel Lord Brudenell's reply.

sixth charges, I am relieved from a very large portion of the difficulty which might, under other circumstances, have occurred; still, after the mass of assertions and long chain of statements which have been adduced, I must say, with as much ingenuity as disregard to correctness of fact, in order to endeavour to establish a case of oppression and ill treatment on my part towards Captain Wathen; I am bound, in justice to myself and my own character, to enter into a detail of refutation, which, I fear, may be irksome to this Court.

"Before I proceed to investigate the evidence adduced in support of the six charges which I have felt it my duty to prefer against Captain Wathen, I shall explain the manner in which they were brought forward by me, as there has been much cavilling on this point. I beg to state to the Court, that on receiving directions from Dublin to frame charges against Captain Wathen, I submitted them to the major-general, who requested that an alteration might be made in one of them: he entirely approved of the first three charges, and said he would willingly come forward as an evidence to substantiate them: of the other three he gave no opinion whatever, they were forwarded to Dublin, and from thence to London, for the consideration of the General commanding-in-chief.

"It has been asked, why the charge for which Captain Wathen was placed in arrest, is made the last. I have only to say, that they are arranged according to dates; the first three charges relate to what occurred on Friday the 8th November; the fourth and fifth to the evening of 8th November, and morning of 9th; the sixth to what occurred on Tuesday the 12th November.

"The prisoner seems to consider it a hardship that no intimation was made to him previous to the 12th November, that charges would be preferred against him for his conduct which has been the ground of the three first charges. Captain Wathen has no reason to complain on this point, as a special report of the extreme impropriety of his conduct on Friday the 8th, and Monday 11th November, was written by the major-general to head-quarters on Tuesday the 12th November, before he became acquainted with the circumstance of Captain Wathen having been placed in arrest for subsequent misconduct.

Lieutenant-Colonel Lord Brudenell's reply.

"I must now commence to narrate circumstances attendant upon, and consequent to, the reading of the general-commanding-in-chief's letter, on the 20th of October last. On that day Major-General Sir Thomas Arbuthnot having read Lord Hill's letter to me at his own house, I told him that I was sorry that there appeared to have been a mistake as to there having been two parades, and that as the adjutant certainly had corrected his error in good time, I hoped he would allow me to say something to the adjutant as to the major-general's good opinion of him in the presence of the other officers of the regiment. The major-general authorized me to tell him that he was fully aware of his zeal, and that he would make a very favourable report of him in his half-yearly inspection report. About an hour after this I received the official letter in question, and at about five o'clock in the afternoon of the same day I read Lord Hill's letter to the officers of the regiment assembled in the mess-room. After having read it, I said, 'The general commanding-in-chief having been pleased to decide upon the differences between Captain Wathen and myself, of course it is not my duty to make any observation thereon; but with regard to the adjutant, I regret that there should have been this misunderstanding relative to there having been two parades on that morning. Mr. Hecker certainly corrected his

Lieutenant-Colonel Lord Brudenell's reply.

error full twenty minutes before the parade. The major-general has authorized me to tell him that he will make a very favourable report of him in his half-yearly inspection report, and that he is fully aware of his zeal.' I added, that I should forward a letter myself to the major-general on the subject, with a request that it might be sent to head-quarters.

"On my honour I can state that this was the tenor, if not the exact words, which I made use of on that occasion, and I did not say one word relative to the past differences between Captain Wathen and myself. I then said, 'Mr. Hecker, Lord Hill's orders will be immediately obeyed, Captain Wathen will be released from arrest.' My own sense of my duty as an officer, and the veneration and respect which I feel for General Lord Hill, both publicly and privately, would have prevented the possibility of my saying any thing which could in the most remote degree have had the appearance of doubting the propriety of his decision.

"I beg to state, that I could bring several officers to prove that I did not give utterance to words in the sense imputed to me by the senior major of this regiment; I shall not think it necessary to give any explanation of my alleged manner and gestures on that occasion, nor will I hazard any opinion on the tone and manner assumed by the senior major in giving his evidence on Thursday last; they were specimens of good taste which I have no doubt will be duly appreciated by this honourable Court; but with reference to another part of his evidence, I cannot but express my extreme surprise that Sir Walter Scott should be so unacquainted with his duty as senior major of this regiment, as to suppose that conversations between him and myself relative to other officers on points of regimental duty, should not be considered confidential, whatever may be his own private feelings of hostility towards me, and of which, until that day, I was totally unaware.

Lieutenant-Colonel Lord Brudenell's reply.

"It appears to me, that under such a system of repeating private conversations of this nature on points of duty, it would be impossible to maintain discipline and harmony in any corps; and if he has all along been acting upon this principle of repeating my observations to officers, it is not surprising that I should have had some difficulties to contend with in the command of the regiment.

"I shall now proceed. When I was at dinner at the regimental mess, at about a quarter past seven o'clock on that day, a letter was brought to me from Captain Wathen, requesting leave of absence to proceed to England. I never felt more surprise in my life, than that an officer whose conduct had scarcely two hours before been strongly animadverted upon in a letter from General Lord Hill, for what his Lordship, in addition to further censure, was pleased to term his unjustifiable conduct towards his commanding officer, should take such an early opportunity of applying for the indulgence of leave of absence; before I refused it, I thought it my duty to acquaint myself with the cause of his application; there are some circumstances under which one could not well refuse an officer leave of absence. By the answer which I received from Captain Wathen, I did not consider his case one of that nature; I therefore refused to grant him leave, assigning, as I thought, sufficient reasons for so doing. I almost immediately afterwards mentioned the circumstance to the major-general, who approved of the course which I had adopted. I told the major-general that when I could only by the regulations of the army in Ireland allow two captains to go on leave, I thought those officers had a prior

Lieutenant-Colonel Lord Brudenell's reply.

claim to the indulgence with whose conduct I was satisfied; and that an officer who had just been reprimanded from head-quarters was not the one I should wish to fix upon. This is the first link in the chain of alleged oppression. And I beg here to state to the Court, that as previous to Captain Wathen's first arrest, I considered my having put his troop in orders on the 5th of September to be the cause of his so frequently thwarting and opposing me, so I consider that my having refused to grant him leave of absence on the 20th of October last, was the real cause of the continuation of that opposition to me as his commanding officer.

"There is also the circumstance of my having written to say that the troop had improved under the subalterns; this, in my opinion, was the case.

"The next charge of oppression is having spoken to Captain Wathen in the field, and ordered him to carry his sword; he having thought proper to sit at ease on his horse during field exercise, and to put his sword in his left hand, and his right arm, [the position was described.] I said, 'Carry your sword properly, Captain Wathen;' he sloped it, and immediately put it back and took up his former position on his horse; this was repeated, as if purposely, several times. I never yet saw any other officer conduct himself in such an extraordinary manner. He also committed several gross mistakes in the command of his squadron. This is the second link in the chain of oppression.

"On the next field-day he trotted past in front of the second file from the left, not in the centre, as he asserts: just a similar fault to an infantry officer putting himself on the left flank in marching past right in front,—a mistake which I imagine would astonish the most inexperienced ensign in this garrison. I certainly spoke to him sharply on that occasion, and what commanding officer would not have done so, or does not occasionally speak sharply in the field? Besides, I had spoken with nearly equal severity to another officer of much less experience, who had committed a similar mistake a short time previously.

Lieutenant-Colonel Lord Brudenell's reply.

" This is the third link.

" The next is the interview between Captain Wathen and myself on the 4th of November ; on that occasion I took the liberty to speak in strong terms to a private hussar of Captain Wathen's troop, of his own carelessness and that of the other men of the troop. I was justified in doing so, I conceive, as the horses of that troop were constantly brought to the parade in an improper state, and there had been in that troop twenty-three sore-backed horses, being very nearly half the number which had existed in all the rest of the regiment since we came to Ireland : and they existed much longer in that troop than in any other. It has been shown in evidence that it is the custom of the regiment for an officer always to attend with a private in the regimental office. I have myself stated in evidence what occurred on that occasion, and the manner in which Captain Wathen insubordinately and disrespectfully told me ' that when I brought such charges against a troop I ought to substantiate them.' As to the assertions made in the prisoner's defence, that I pointed to the ground and said, ' Come back, sir,' accompanied by many harsh terms, the whole are unfounded in fact. Lieutenant and Adjutant Hecker states, in answer to a question from the prosecutor, that Captain Wathen, on returning to the regimental office, said, ' When you, Lord Brudenell, make such statements respecting my troop, you should bear them out.'

Lieutenant-Colonel Lord Brudenell's reply.

" In answer to the following question, ' Do you recollect what I said to Captain Wathen on that occasion ?'—evidence answers, ' Lord Brudenell said he did consider Captain Wathen's manner improper in addressing him in the way he had done ;' that ' Captain Wathen then said, that he was not aware that his manner had been improper.'

" In answer to the next question from prisoner—' Do you recollect what Lord Brudenell said immediately in reply ?' Answer, ' I do not.' Now I beg to ask whether it is possible that the adjutant could have forgotten the circumstance of such violent language as is attributed to me in the prisoner's defence ? Sir, I deny the correctness of that statement; and with reference to that part of the conversation which is stated to have occurred in private Surrett's presence, why was not private Surrett called in to give evidence ? I have a right to suppose that Captain Wathen knew that private Surrett could not substantiate the accusation, he therefore avoided calling upon him, preferring to make assertions on his defence.

" I must here digress from the direct course of alleged oppression to another accusation brought against me, viz. that of having kept Captain Wathen under close arrest at the commencement of each of the arrests. I cannot avoid saying that I heard with indignation this unfounded charge brought against me. Some days after Captain Wathen was placed in arrest, he applied to me, through the adjutant, to know whether he was under close arrest ? I immediately answered that of course he was not, and that he might take exercise. I now ask why he did not apply to me immediately on this subject ? I have as much right to say that he delayed to do so for the sake of having an opportunity of bringing a charge of oppression against me,

Lieutenant Colonel Lord Brudenell's reply.

as he has to assert that I intentionally kept him under close arrest for some days. On the occasion of his first arrest, the first order I gave was, that he might take two hours' exercise. I almost immediately afterwards, on reconsideration, directed the adjutant to write to say that he might take what exercise he pleased. Once when a regiment was formed on parade, and Captain Wathen was walking with some officers, the adjutant was directed by me to tell him, that under all circumstances of his being in arrest, I did not think he was doing quite right. Be this as it may, I have constantly since seen him walking with officers both of other regiments and his own, and I have never interfered with him in any way; and he has had, from the commencement of his arrest up to the present day, full liberty of taking exercise, and has never, by my orders, been deprived of the society of his friends; therefore his assertions on this point are contrary to fact.

"With reference to the senior major being appointed president of a regimental Court-Martial, on Monday, the 11th of November, I beg to state that I have more than once appointed field-officers for that duty, and that as on this occasion there were so few subalterns at head-quarters, that I was obliged to put a Captain as a member, there was nothing which could strike any person as extraordinary in that measure; the only injurious result which could arise, was from Sir Walter Scott repeating my observations to the officer, who, for reasons which I am about to assign, I did not wish to appoint. The case to be tried was in some measure an intricate one, and required that I should previously confer with the president. Captain Wathen had on the previous Friday been guilty of conduct for which I have since preferred two charges for conduct unbecoming

Lieutenant-Colonel Lord Brudenell's reply.

the character of an officer and a gentleman. I never, to my recollection, on that occasion, said that his mind was affected; I said that his conduct had been most extraordinary and improper; and I myself knew that it was still under the consideration of the major-general.

"The following has appeared in the defence:—'I believe it to be the present understanding of the Court, from what was stated in the prosecution, that the demur made by private Hopkins was to the expense of repairing his jacket, whereas it was not so; but to be furnished with a new one when the old one was repairable.' I have already stated, in evidence, the circumstances of this case: and I must now again positively contradict the statement in the defence; and further I beg to state, that private Hopkins did not make the complaint about the repairs of his jacket till Sunday, the 10th of November, two days after Captain Wathen's representations to the major-general about the discontent of his men—the men had then a good example set them of grumbling. I conclude, the reason that private Hopkins was not called in to substantiate this statement was, that he is too good a soldier to state what is contrary to truth.

"I shall not think it necessary to explain the circumstance of the stable-jacket stated to have been thrown towards private Hopkins on parade; that and many other equally frivolous accusations of the sort only exhibit the weakness of the cause in aid of which they are adduced.

1st Charge.

"I shall now proceed to introduce to the Court the principal points in the evidence in support of the three first charges.

Sir Thomas Arbuthnot's evidence.

"On Captain Wathen saying, 'I understand Lieutenant-Colonel Lord Brudenell has made a complaint to you respecting the amount of the debt of my troop,' Sir Thomas

Arbuthnot replies, 'Lord Brudenell has made no such complaint, and I know nothing of the matter; and I must say that it does appear strange to me that you should surmise such a thing of your commanding officer.'

Lieutenant-Colonel Lord Brudenell's reply.

"Captain Wathen then stated that the amount of his troop debt had been created by an unusual supply of stable-jackets which had been sent to him from the tailor's shop; he did not know by whose order or for what purpose.

"Captain Corkran states:—

"'Captain Wathen stated that an unusual number of stable-jackets had been issued to the men of his troop, he scarcely knew why or by whose authority.'

1st Charge. Captain Corkran.

"Lieutenant and Adjutant Hecker's testimony and the prosecutor's testimony have been also given in support of this charge.

1st Charge. Lieutenant Adjutant Hecker; Prosecutor.

"In answer to a question from the major-general whether the supply had been an unusual one, Captain Wathen's reply was, 'Yes, Sir, I can prove it by my ledger; and the supply of them has created much discontent amongst the men of my troop.'

2nd Charge. Sir T. Arbuthnot.

"After further remarks, the major-general said, 'All this, Sir, appears to me very extraordinary, but as you stated that discontent was created amongst your men by the issue of the jackets in question, pray let me know if you reported the circumstance to your commanding officer.' Captain Wathen replied, 'Yes, Sir, I did,' on which Lord Brudenell, in a hasty manner, said, 'I positively deny that Captain Wathen ever made such a report to me.' In a tone of surprise, I then repeated the question to Captain Wathen, and on his stating that he had made such a report to his commanding officer, Lord Brudenell said, 'Sir, it is fal—.'

"The major-general afterwards states, 'I sent for all the commanding officers of troops, viz. Captains Rose, M'Queen,

Lieutenant-Colonel Lord Brudenell's reply.

Ives, and Wood. To these officers I put the question, if the late issue of jackets for the men of the troops under their command was an unusual one, and if such had created discontent. The reply from each of them was in the negative. I then remarked, Captain Wathen, it does appear to me extremely strange that the men of your troop alone should be discontented on this subject, &c.; when, to my surprise, Captain Wathen, in a very abrupt and disrespectful manner, as it appeared to me, said, 'Sir I did not say so;' on which I remarked, 'Surely Captain Wathen, you cannot deny it;' and I appealed to Lord Brudenell, my aide-de-camp, and the adjutant of the regiment, if you did not state the issue of jackets in question was an unusual one, and that such had created discontent among your men; they each of them replied positively in the affirmative. On this Captain Wathen remarked, 'Really, Sir, my mind was so irritated and my feelings were such at having yesterday been 'taunted' by my commanding officer respecting the amount of my troop debt, that I may have said some things for which I cannot now account.'

"I shall shortly show, by the evidence given to this Court, that Captain Wathen had no cause whatever to be irritated or excited by any thing which had occurred on the previous day in the regimental office.

"I shall first narrate the remainder of the major-general's most important testimony, viz.:—

"'Shortly after my arrival in the barrack yard on Monday, the 11th, I sent for Captain Wathen, &c. When Captain Wathen came, I requested he would send for the serjeants of his troop, he having informed me, on the Friday preceding, that the serjeants had told him of the discontent of the men respecting the issue of the stable-jackets in question;' on which Captain Wathen said, 'General, you may recollect that I denied the other day that the serjeants had given me any such information; pardon me, you must have misunderstood me.' I replied, 'You positively said so; and I appeal to Lord Brudenell and my aide-de-camp if you did not say so; both of whom said yes.'

Lieutenant-Colonel Lord Brudenell's reply.

"On cross-examination, Sir T. Arbuthnot states:—

On cross-examination, Sir T. Arbuthnot.

"'On the 11th of November I sent for Captain Wathen, and when he came, I requested that he would bring forward those serjeants who had informed him that the men of his troop were discontented at the issue of the stable-jackets in question. Captain Wathen then said, 'Sir, you may recollect that I denied the other day that the serjeants had given me any such information, or that the men were discontented; pardon me, General, you must have misunderstood.' My remark was, 'Captain Wathen, I could not have misunderstood you; you certainly made the denial you mentioned, and this I must say was done in a most improper and insubordinate manner.'

"In answer to another question, the major-general states,—

"'When Captain Wathen, on the 8th of November, informed me that discontent existed amongst some of his men, respecting the issue of the stable-jackets, I requested him to let me know, how this came to his knowledge; he hesitated for some time in making a reply, (and I beg leave to call the particular attention of the Court to this part of the major-general's evidence,) when I pointed out to him that it was impossible for me to allow a matter of such a nature to remain without explanation.' I said, Captain Wathen, I must insist upon your telling me who gave you this information. He then stated, 'his serjeants.'

"To the following question of the prisoner, viz.

"'Immediately, on understanding that you conceived I had said that my men had complained, and that I had

Question from prisoner.

Lieutenant-Colonel Lord Brudenell's reply.

Answer.

heard so from my serjeants ; did I not express my wish to remove that opinion from your mind ?'

" The major-general answers. ' No, you appeared to me to persevere in those assertions, till you denied them in the abrupt manner already alluded to, before the commanding officers of troops.'

" Now I beg to point out to the Court, that I have, upon my own sworn testimony, stated that a parade under arms intervened between Captain Wathen's statement, on the 8th of November, to the major-general, relative to the discontent of his men, which had been told to him by his serjeants, and which he said he had reported, or mentioned to his commanding officer; and the assembling of the captains of troops in the office by the major-general's order. This fact was corroborated by Captain Rose in his evidence on the defence on Tuesday last, when in answer to a question from prosecutor, whether it was not dark when the major-general left the regimental-office, after the interview with the captains of troops, Captain Rose states, ' Yes, it was dark.' By the above chain of evidence, it must be evident to this honourable Court, that a very considerable space of time—I have, on my sworn testimony, stated, about an hour—must have intervened between Captain Wathen's statement, relative to the discontent of his men, and his first denial of it in the presence of the captains of troops.

" Prosecutor's evidence on this point was as follows, viz. " I accompanied the major-general to a parade under arms of the regiment in the barrack-yard ; shortly after the parade Captain Wathen was sent for again to the regimental-office, which was about one hour from the time of his having made the above statement. The major-general then told him that it was his duty to make particular inquiries into the subject of the discontent of his men ; upon which Captain Wathen told him he had never said his men were discontented. The major-general reminded him that he had said, that the serjeants had reported to him that the men were discontented ; upon which Captain Wathen, in a very disrespectful manner gave a flat denial to the major-general. About this time the captains of troops were sent for to the orderly-room,' &c.

Lieutenant-Colonel Lord Brudenell's reply.

" In answer to the following question from the Court, viz.—

Question.

" ' Do you imagine Captain Wathen made the statement to you wilfully, or that his irritated feelings may have caused the misrepresentation he made on the 8th of November, and which he was so anxious to correct ?' the major-general replies, ' Wilfully, actuated by his irritated feelings.'

Answer.

" ' When you say wilfully, do you wish the Court to understand that Captain Wathen's irritation induced him to make a representation knowing it to be false ?

2nd Question.

" ' Captain Wathen's statement, in my estimation, was wilful and decided ; his irritated feelings may have bereft him of the power of reasoning on the subject at the time.'

Answer.

In answer to a question from the Court on the same subject, Captain Corkran replies, ' I think he was capable of exercising his judgment.'

Captain Corkran.

" The fact of Captain Wathen having reported to the major-general that his men were discontented, and that the serjeants had reported the circumstance to him is corroborated by Captain Corkran, and Lieutenant and Adjutant Hecker, in addition to the testimony of the prosecutor. Colonel Turner has also corroborated the circumstances

Lieutenant-Colonel Lord Brudenell's reply.

which occurred in the regimental office, after the parade under arms on the 8th instant, when Captain Wathen denied, in the positive and abrupt manner already described, that he had made the above-named statements to the major-general relative to the discontent of the men.

1st Charge.

"Relative to the first charge, Captain Corkran has given the following evidence, in answer to a question by the Court, as to whether he conceived Captain Wathen meant to make a report against his commanding officer, and thereby imputing improper conduct to him, when he Captain Wathen spoke to the major-general about the amount of the troop debt, viz.

Answer.

"'I certainly thought that it was an indirect accusation against his commanding officer.'

"I beg here to point out that Captains Blythe and Wood, and Quarter-Master Chettle, have in their evidence proved that it has been the custom of this regiment to issue new stable-jackets to the men as they may require them, and Colonels Clarke and Chatterton, that it is the custom in the cavalry service.

"Captain Wood, who did duty in Captain Wathen's troop, has proved that the stable-jackets were first rejected openly on parade, and therefore it must have been known to every person in the regiment by whose orders the new jackets were issued.

3rd Charge.

"Prosecutor has stated positively, on oath, 'that Captain Wathen never did report or mention to him that the men of Captain Wathen's troop were discontented.'

7th November.

"I beg now to call the attention of the Court to the circumstance which occurred at the interview of the 7th of November between Captain Wathen and myself, when, as it has already appeared, in Major-General Sir Thomas Arbuthnot's evidence, Captain Wathen stated on the 8th of November, that I had so 'taunted' him with his troop debt as to put him into an unusual state of irritation.

Lieutenant-Colonel Lord Brudenell's reply.

" Lieutenant and Adjutant Hecker has stated in evidence, viz., 'I heard no harsh words applied to Captain Wathen by Lord Brudenell on the 8th of November; the morning before the inspection on the 8th of November, there was a conversation in the regimental office between Captain Wathen and Lord Brudenell respecting the excess of his troop debt. Captain Wathen was asked by Lord Brudenell the reason why his troop debt was so large. Captain Wathen stated in reply, that numerous articles had been issued out to the men of his troop which had been entered in his ledger, and had increased the amount of his debt. Reference was then made by Lord Brudenell to the debt of another troop, which was considerably lower than Captain Wathen's.'

Lieutenant and Adjutant Hecker.

" Captain Wathen answered that he was responsible only for his own debt, and that perhaps the troop debt to which allusion had been made, was small in consequence of the articles which had been issued out to that troop not being charged in the ledger.

Answer.

" 'Did I speak harshly to him on that occasion, or in the tone of a reprimand?'

Question from prosecutor.

" 'No, I did not consider it so.'

Answer.

" Prosecutor stated in giving evidence in answer to a question from the prisoner, viz.:

Prosecutor.

" Did I not tell the major-general you had warned me I should have to explain the cause of my debt?'

Question.

" 'Captain Wathen did so, but I never had warned him to that effect.'

Answer.

" Lieutenant and Adjutant Hecker, in answer to a question from the Court—

Lieutenant and Adjutant Hecker.

Lieutenant-Colonel Lord Brudenell's reply.

Question.

" 'Did you hear Captain Wathen, when his books were examined, tell Sir Thomas Arbuthnot that Lieutenant-Colonel Lord Brudenell had warned him on the previous day that he should have to account to him, the major-general, for the excess of his troop debt?'

Answer.

" 'I do not recollect his having done so.'

Lieutenant and Adjutant Hecker.

" The following question was also put to Lieutenant and Adjutant Hecker, viz:—

" 'When the conversation took place in the regimental office between Captain Wathen and Lord Brudenell on the morning before the 8th of November, 1833, did Lord Brudenell express himself to Captain Wathen in his ordinary tone of voice and manner while speaking to the officers of the 15th Hussars?'

Answer.

" 'Lord Brudenell's voice was raised above the ordinary tone.'

" This, I fear, has too often been the case in the presence of this honourable Court; and this is the cause assigned by Captain Wathen himself for his alleged excitement on the 8th of November last. Far, Sir, I should conceive from a sufficient excuse for an officer, twenty-four hours afterwards, deliberately making statements to a general officer at the half-yearly inspection of a regiment, directly contrary to truth and fact.

" As to the harsh terms in which I am accused in the prisoner's written defence of having addressed him at the interview in question—the accusation, like the greater part of the others contained in that document, is quite unfounded in fact.

" The three first charges I now consider clearly established, as Captain Wathen's bare assertion, unsupported by any proof, cannot be taken as evidence to invalidate facts proved by the testimony of the Major-general, Captain Corkran, Colonel Turner, the adjutant, and myself, in support of these charges; and here I must beg to point out the extreme inconsistency of Captain Wathen's assertions throughout. At one moment he declares he was in such a state of excitement and agitation as not to be aware of what he said or did, although at the same time his memory was so extremely clear and retentive that he pretends to recollect all that occurred on that occasion, and on his sole testimony expects to establish that five witnesses were mistaken.

Lieutenant-Colonel Lord Brudenell's reply.

"If, as I conceive to be the case, these charges are proved, there can be little doubt of the prisoner's conduct being unbecoming the character of an officer and a gentleman.

Fourth Charge.

"The main points of the fourth charge I likewise consider clearly proved, as Captain Wathen has not even attempted to explain away his having officially reported to me that he had assembled his men after evening stables, on the 8th of November, when such was not the fact; and although it appears from the testimony of two out of four non-commissioned officers, who, a fortnight or three weeks after the circumstances occurred, suddenly remembered that Captain Wathen had spoken to the men in their stables, a fact which at the time they all repeatedly denied, I see no reason to doubt the testimony of Serjeant Denby and Corporal Mackay; for although Captain Wathen had warned twelve privates as witnesses, he found it expedient only to produce one, private Young; therefore admitting the evidence of the one private to be correct against that of the two non-commissioned officers, there still remain two stables wholly unaccounted for, which clearly proves that

Lieutenant-Colonel Lord Brudenell's reply.

if the order was obeyed, it was in a partial and irregular manner.

"An accusation of unfairness has been brought against me, for not having notified to Captain Wathen that this charge was to be brought against him. This is very easily accounted for. I had no reason to believe that he had neglected to obey the order conveyed to him by the adjutant on the 8th of November, until after I received his official letter of the 12th of November, which was sent to me some time after he had been placed in arrest. Was it to be expected that I should make any communication to him on this one point, when I well knew, that if I was ordered to prefer charges at all, I should have to prefer several against him?

"The prisoner, totally disregarding Lieutenant and Adjutant Hecker's testimony on oath, states that he, Captain Wathen, was the only captain of a troop who obeyed the order.

"It has been urged in the prisoner's defence, that I must have been perfectly aware, when I committed this charge to paper, that if he had not read the orders to the men on the evening in question, that he would not have neglected a duty, nor disobeyed an order.

"Captain Wathen was not ordered to read the orders to the men. In conformity to the major-general's orders given to me, officers commanding troops were directed to communicate verbally to their men the major-general's approbation. My written regimental orders referred to many other matters; and the reading of them according to custom, by the orderly officer, did not at all supersede the necessity of the major-general's orders being obeyed.

"Captain Wathen also expresses surprise that I should

doubt his written statement; I had unfortunately, at this time, very strong reasons for doubting both his verbal and written statements.

Lieutenant-Colonel Lord Brudenell's reply.

"The statement in his official letter of the 12th of November, relative to his having assembled his men after evening stables on the 8th of November, is clearly at variance with truth and fact.

Fifth charge.

"There can be no doubt, I conceive, that the fifth charge is, by the evidence adduced, distinctly proved, as far as Captain Wathen having addressed his troop in a very irregular and unofficerlike manner, corroborating the fact of the language having been used, which I attributed to him in the charge.

"I will not repeat the testimony of the four non-commissioned officers called as evidences.

"Three out of four of them have sworn that Captain Wathen referred to previous unpleasant circumstances, viz., 'notwithstanding unpleasant circumstances which had occurred.'

"Now, the prisoner states that I had told private Surrett in his, Captain Wathen's presence, that in consequence of the irregularities in the troop, it was the worst in the regiment; he admits that he had constantly found fault with his troop on parade; yet in defiance of this, the confirmed and repeatedly expressed opinion of his commanding officer, he assembles his men at an irregular hour; he tells them that the left troop of the line was particularly admired by civilians and strangers; that if they went on service, they would be as brave a troop as any other troop and would do their duty as well as any other in the service, notwithstanding unpleasant circumstances which had occurred. It is true, that only one non-commissioned offi-

Lieutenant-Colonel Lord Brudenell's reply.

cer has connected this reference to unpleasant circumstances with any precise previous circumstance.

"Serjeant-Major Thom states in evidence, that he considered it alluded to Captain Wathen's first arrest, which would have been an equally improper allusion on the part of Captain Wathen; but notwithstanding the absence of more direct evidence with regard to this part of the charge, this honourable Court will, I feel convinced, consider, after all that has been made known to them relative to this troop during these proceedings, that such an address could not have been made with any good feeling towards his commanding officer, or with any other intention than that of taking an independent line with regard to his troop, by expressing opinions in direct opposition to those of his commanding officer, to the prejudice of good order, and the discipline of the regiment.

"What was the cause of this address, as assigned by himself? Because a few men had turned out with their horses not quite so well dressed as usual, (he is pleased to state, in direct opposition to the opinion of his commanding officer,) for which he himself has assigned two very sufficient reasons to the Court, namely, the late field-day on the previous day, and the late indulgence which the men had received from me on the previous evening, all of which circumstances he was perfectly well aware of, when he went on parade that morning.

"I beg to state, that as commanding officer of the regiment, I did not find fault with any man or horse on parade that morning.

"With referance to an allusion in the written defence of the prisoner, to Lance-Serjeant Denby having been particularly questioned by me because I knew that he was ill affected towards his commanding officer, I have only to say, that I never knew, nor do I know now, that either Lance-Serjeant Denby, or any other non-commissioned officer, or even private, is ill affected towards his captain.

Lieutenant-Colonel Lord Brudenell's reply.

"Lance-Serjeant Denby did not come to me oftener than the other non-commissioned officers of the troop on this business. If he came first, which was probably the case, it was, I conceive, by chance, being nearest at hand at the time.

"I have no further observations to offer on this charge; which I must consider as distinctly proved.

Sixth charge.

"There can be no doubt of the repeated disobedience of orders being distinctly proved against the prisoner in the sixth charge. The prisoner has urged in defence of his conduct that the order was unlawful; and the senior major, who had not the quickness to observe this alleged illegality at the time, has offered the same opinion. I beg to state that, in my own opinion, I cannot possibly consider it an unlawful order. It is proved that the document was not to be taken as a finished one. Captain Wathen should have obeyed my orders: he might have protested against any injurious result which might afterwards arise to himself, if he could have anticipated any thing of the sort; but I conceive that there is no order which an officer and soldier must not obey, except one which would render the person obeying it amenable to the civil laws of his country. Were the principle of soldiers being the judges of what orders they are to obey once admitted, discipline would soon be subverted, and there would soon be regiments of lawyers instead of obedient soldiers.

"Had Captain Wathen requested me in a proper manner to take the document away with him, I should probably have acceded to his request; instead of which he com-

Lieutenant-Colonel Lord Brudenell's reply.

menced by refusing to obey my order in a decided manner, and he continued to decline to obey it in the same positive manner.

"With reference to evidence brought before the Court, I beg to state that I did not send for the senior major to give advice to Captain Wathen, but to be witness to his repeated disobedience of orders; as commanding officer of a regiment, I do not, I conceive, require the assistance of others to enforce obedience to my orders; and as 'to my having willingly seized upon an opportunity to place Captain Wathen in arrest,' as has been stated, the length of time which this interview continued, the repeated refusal of Captain Wathen to obey my orders, and the manner in which I have shown that I endeavoured almost to persuade him to obey my orders, must be my justification on this point.

"I think that this honourable Court will now consider that each and every one of the charges, which I have felt it my duty to prefer against Captain Wathen, is proved.

"I do not wish to speak with unnecessary harshness; but I must say, that veracity being the first qualification of a gentleman, and obedience to orders that of an officer, that this officer has deliberately outraged both.

"This honourable Court will, I think, consider the whole of such conduct as aforesaid insubordinate, unbecoming the character of an officer and a gentleman, to the prejudice of good order and military discipline, and in breach of the Articles of War.

"With reference to the last charge, as it has been stated that the taking down Captain Wathen's words in the office was improper, I cannot venture any opinion on that point in presence of this honourable Court. I beg to state that it is the only occasion on which an officer's words